THE
BOOK
OF
PROVERBS

With 10 Reflections from
Our Daily Bread.

NEW INTERNATIONAL VERSION

ZONDERVAN®

NIV The Book of Proverbs, with 10 Reflections from Our Daily Bread®
Published by Zondervan
Grand Rapids, Michigan 49546, USA
www.zondervan.com

Printed in the United States of America

17 18 19 20 21 22 23 24 25 /DPM/ 14 13 12 11 10 9 8 7 6 5 4 3 2

A portion of the purchase price of your NIV® Bible is provided to Biblica so together we support the mission of *Transforming lives through God's Word.*

Biblica provides God's Word to people through translation, publishing and Bible engagement in Africa, Asia Pacific, Europe, Latin America, Middle East, and North America. Through its worldwide reach, Biblica engages people with God's Word so that their lives are transformed through a relationship with Jesus Christ.

THE
BOOK
OF
PROVERBS

Purpose and Theme

1 The proverbs of Solomon son of David, king of Israel:

²for gaining wisdom and instruction;
    for understanding words of insight;
³for receiving instruction in prudent behavior,
    doing what is right and just and fair;
⁴for giving prudence to those who are simple,ᵃ
    knowledge and discretion to the young—
⁵let the wise listen and add to their learning,
    and let the discerning get guidance—
⁶for understanding proverbs and parables,
    the sayings and riddles of the wise.ᵇ

⁷The fear of the LORD is the beginning of knowledge,
    but foolsᶜ despise wisdom and instruction.

Prologue: Exhortations to Embrace Wisdom

Warning Against the Invitation of Sinful Men

⁸Listen, my son, to your father's instruction
    and do not forsake your mother's teaching.

ᵃ 4 The Hebrew word rendered *simple* in Proverbs denotes a person who is gullible, without moral direction and inclined to evil.   ᵇ 6 Or *understanding a proverb, namely, a parable, / and the sayings of the wise, their riddles*   ᶜ 7 The Hebrew words rendered *fool* in Proverbs, and often elsewhere in the Old Testament, denote a person who is morally deficient.

⁹They are a garland to grace your head
  and a chain to adorn your neck.

¹⁰My son, if sinful men entice you,
  do not give in to them.
¹¹If they say, "Come along with us;
  let's lie in wait for innocent blood,
  let's ambush some harmless soul;
¹²let's swallow them alive, like the grave,
  and whole, like those who go down to the pit;
¹³we will get all sorts of valuable things
  and fill our houses with plunder;
¹⁴cast lots with us;
  we will all share the loot" —
¹⁵my son, do not go along with them,
  do not set foot on their paths;
¹⁶for their feet rush into evil,
  they are swift to shed blood.
¹⁷How useless to spread a net
  where every bird can see it!
¹⁸These men lie in wait for their own blood;
  they ambush only themselves!
¹⁹Such are the paths of all who go after ill-gotten gain;
  it takes away the life of those who get it.

Wisdom's Rebuke

²⁰Out in the open wisdom calls aloud,
  she raises her voice in the public square;
²¹on top of the wall[a] she cries out,
  at the city gate she makes her speech:

---

[a] 21 Septuagint; Hebrew / at noisy street corners

²²"How long will you who are simple love your simple
  ways?
How long will mockers delight in mockery
  and fools hate knowledge?
²³Repent at my rebuke!
Then I will pour out my thoughts to you,
  I will make known to you my teachings.
²⁴But since you refuse to listen when I call
  and no one pays attention when I stretch out
    my hand,
²⁵since you disregard all my advice
  and do not accept my rebuke,
²⁶I in turn will laugh when disaster strikes you;
  I will mock when calamity overtakes you—
²⁷when calamity overtakes you like a storm,
  when disaster sweeps over you like a whirlwind,
  when distress and trouble overwhelm you.

²⁸"Then they will call to me but I will not answer;
  they will look for me but will not find me,
²⁹since they hated knowledge
  and did not choose to fear the LORD.
³⁰Since they would not accept my advice
  and spurned my rebuke,
³¹they will eat the fruit of their ways
  and be filled with the fruit of their schemes.
³²For the waywardness of the simple will kill them,
  and the complacency of fools will destroy them;
³³but whoever listens to me will live in safety
  and be at ease, without fear of harm."

Moral Benefits of Wisdom

2 My son, if you accept my words
and store up my commands within you,
² turning your ear to wisdom
and applying your heart to understanding —
³ indeed, if you call out for insight
and cry aloud for understanding,
⁴ and if you look for it as for silver
and search for it as for hidden treasure,
⁵ then you will understand the fear of the LORD
and find the knowledge of God.
⁶ For the LORD gives wisdom;
from his mouth come knowledge and understanding.
⁷ He holds success in store for the upright,
he is a shield to those whose walk is blameless,
⁸ for he guards the course of the just
and protects the way of his faithful ones.

⁹ Then you will understand what is right and just
and fair — every good path.
¹⁰ For wisdom will enter your heart,
and knowledge will be pleasant to your soul.
¹¹ Discretion will protect you,
and understanding will guard you.

¹² Wisdom will save you from the ways of wicked men,
from men whose words are perverse,
¹³ who have left the straight paths
to walk in dark ways,
¹⁴ who delight in doing wrong
and rejoice in the perverseness of evil,
¹⁵ whose paths are crooked
and who are devious in their ways.

Hidden Treasure

If you look for [wisdom] as for silver and search for it as for hidden treasure, then you will understand the fear of the LORD.
PROVERBS 2:4-5

My husband and I read in different ways. Since English is a second language for Tom, he has a tendency to read slowly, word-for-word. I often speed-read by skimming. But Tom retains more than I do. He can easily quote something he read a week ago, while my retention can evaporate seconds after I turn away from the screen or book.

Skimming is also a problem when I'm reading the Bible—and not just the genealogies. I'm tempted to skim familiar passages, stories I've heard since I was a child or a psalm that is part of a familiar chorus.

Proverbs 2 encourages us to make the effort to know God better by carefully seeking a heart of understanding. When we read the Bible carefully and invest time memorizing Scripture, we absorb its truths more deeply (vv. 1–2). Sometimes reading the Word aloud helps us to hear and understand the wisdom of God more fully. And when we pray the words of Scripture back to God and ask Him for "insight" and "understanding" (v. 3), we can enjoy a conversation with the Author.

We come to know God and His wisdom when we search for it with our whole heart. We find understanding when we seek it like silver and search for it like hidden treasure.

—CINDY HESS KASPER

Read the Bible carefully and study it prayerfully.

¹⁶Wisdom will save you also from the adulterous woman,
    from the wayward woman with her seductive words,
¹⁷who has left the partner of her youth
    and ignored the covenant she made before God.^a
¹⁸Surely her house leads down to death
    and her paths to the spirits of the dead.
¹⁹None who go to her return
    or attain the paths of life.

²⁰Thus you will walk in the ways of the good
    and keep to the paths of the righteous.
²¹For the upright will live in the land,
    and the blameless will remain in it;
²²but the wicked will be cut off from the land,
    and the unfaithful will be torn from it.

Wisdom Bestows Well-Being

3 My son, do not forget my teaching,
    but keep my commands in your heart,
²for they will prolong your life many years
    and bring you peace and prosperity.

³Let love and faithfulness never leave you;
    bind them around your neck,
    write them on the tablet of your heart.
⁴Then you will win favor and a good name
    in the sight of God and man.

⁵Trust in the LORD with all your heart
    and lean not on your own understanding;
⁶in all your ways submit to him,
    and he will make your paths straight.^b

---

^a 17 Or *covenant of her God*   ^b 6 Or *will direct your paths*

God's Direction

In all your ways submit to [the LORD], and he will make your paths straight.
PROVERBS 3:6

A little more than a century ago, forty-one-year-old Oswald Chambers arrived in Egypt to serve as a YMCA chaplain to British Commonwealth troops during World War I. He was assigned to a camp at Zeitoun, six miles north of Cairo. On his first night there, October 27, 1915, Chambers wrote in his diary, "This [area] is absolutely desert in the very heart of the troops and a glorious opportunity for men. It is all immensely unlike anything I have been used to, and I am watching with interest the new things God will do and engineer."

Chambers believed and practiced the words of Proverbs 3:5–6: "Trust in the LORD with all your heart and lean not on your own understanding; in all your ways submit to him, and he will make your paths straight" (3:5–6).

This is both a comfort and a challenge. There is security in knowing that the Lord will lead us each day, but we must not become so attached to our plans that we resist God's redirection or His timing.

"We have no right to judge where we should be put, or to have preconceived notions as to what God is fitting us for," said Chambers. "God engineers everything. Wherever He puts us, our one great aim is to pour out a whole-hearted devotion to Him in that particular work."

—DAVID McCASLAND

As we trust in God, He directs our steps.

⁷Do not be wise in your own eyes;
    fear the L<small>ORD</small> and shun evil.
⁸This will bring health to your body
    and nourishment to your bones.

⁹Honor the L<small>ORD</small> with your wealth,
    with the firstfruits of all your crops;
¹⁰then your barns will be filled to overflowing,
    and your vats will brim over with new wine.

¹¹My son, do not despise the L<small>ORD</small>'s discipline,
    and do not resent his rebuke,
¹²because the L<small>ORD</small> disciplines those he loves,
    as a father the son he delights in.ᵃ

¹³Blessed are those who find wisdom,
    those who gain understanding,
¹⁴for she is more profitable than silver
    and yields better returns than gold.
¹⁵She is more precious than rubies;
    nothing you desire can compare with her.
¹⁶Long life is in her right hand;
    in her left hand are riches and honor.
¹⁷Her ways are pleasant ways,
    and all her paths are peace.
¹⁸She is a tree of life to those who take hold of her;
    those who hold her fast will be blessed.

¹⁹By wisdom the L<small>ORD</small> laid the earth's foundations,
    by understanding he set the heavens in place;
²⁰by his knowledge the watery depths were divided,
    and the clouds let drop the dew.

ᵃ 12 Hebrew; Septuagint *loves, / and he chastens everyone he accepts as his child*

²¹ My son, do not let wisdom and understanding out of
    your sight,
  preserve sound judgment and discretion;
²² they will be life for you,
    an ornament to grace your neck.
²³ Then you will go on your way in safety,
    and your foot will not stumble.
²⁴ When you lie down, you will not be afraid;
    when you lie down, your sleep will be sweet.
²⁵ Have no fear of sudden disaster
    or of the ruin that overtakes the wicked,
²⁶ for the LORD will be at your side
    and will keep your foot from being snared.

²⁷ Do not withhold good from those to whom it is due,
    when it is in your power to act.
²⁸ Do not say to your neighbor,
    "Come back tomorrow and I'll give it to you" —
    when you already have it with you.
²⁹ Do not plot harm against your neighbor,
    who lives trustfully near you.
³⁰ Do not accuse anyone for no reason —
    when they have done you no harm.

³¹ Do not envy the violent
    or choose any of their ways.

³² For the LORD detests the perverse
    but takes the upright into his confidence.
³³ The LORD's curse is on the house of the wicked,
    but he blesses the home of the righteous.
³⁴ He mocks proud mockers
    but shows favor to the humble and oppressed.

³⁵The wise inherit honor,
  but fools get only shame.

Get Wisdom at Any Cost

4 Listen, my sons, to a father's instruction;
  pay attention and gain understanding.
²I give you sound learning,
  so do not forsake my teaching.
³For I too was a son to my father,
  still tender, and cherished by my mother.
⁴Then he taught me, and he said to me,
  "Take hold of my words with all your heart;
  keep my commands, and you will live.
⁵Get wisdom, get understanding;
  do not forget my words or turn away from them.
⁶Do not forsake wisdom, and she will protect you;
  love her, and she will watch over you.
⁷The beginning of wisdom is this: Get[a] wisdom.
  Though it cost all you have,[b] get understanding.
⁸Cherish her, and she will exalt you;
  embrace her, and she will honor you.
⁹She will give you a garland to grace your head
  and present you with a glorious crown."

¹⁰Listen, my son, accept what I say,
  and the years of your life will be many.
¹¹I instruct you in the way of wisdom
  and lead you along straight paths.
¹²When you walk, your steps will not be hampered;
  when you run, you will not stumble.

---

[a] 7 Or *Wisdom is supreme; therefore get*   [b] 7 Or *wisdom. / Whatever else you get*

[13]Hold on to instruction, do not let it go;
  guard it well, for it is your life.
[14]Do not set foot on the path of the wicked
  or walk in the way of evildoers.
[15]Avoid it, do not travel on it;
  turn from it and go on your way.
[16]For they cannot rest until they do evil;
  they are robbed of sleep till they make someone
    stumble.
[17]They eat the bread of wickedness
  and drink the wine of violence.

[18]The path of the righteous is like the morning sun,
  shining ever brighter till the full light of day.
[19]But the way of the wicked is like deep darkness;
  they do not know what makes them stumble.

[20]My son, pay attention to what I say;
  turn your ear to my words.
[21]Do not let them out of your sight,
  keep them within your heart;
[22]for they are life to those who find them
  and health to one's whole body.
[23]Above all else, guard your heart,
  for everything you do flows from it.
[24]Keep your mouth free of perversity;
  keep corrupt talk far from your lips.
[25]Let your eyes look straight ahead;
  fix your gaze directly before you.
[26]Give careful thought to the[a] paths for your feet
  and be steadfast in all your ways.

---

[a] 26 Or *Make level*

²⁷Do not turn to the right or the left;
  keep your foot from evil.

Warning Against Adultery

5 My son, pay attention to my wisdom,
  turn your ear to my words of insight,
²that you may maintain discretion
  and your lips may preserve knowledge.
³For the lips of the adulterous woman drip honey,
  and her speech is smoother than oil;
⁴but in the end she is bitter as gall,
  sharp as a double-edged sword.
⁵Her feet go down to death;
  her steps lead straight to the grave.
⁶She gives no thought to the way of life;
  her paths wander aimlessly, but she does not know it.

⁷Now then, my sons, listen to me;
  do not turn aside from what I say.
⁸Keep to a path far from her,
  do not go near the door of her house,
⁹lest you lose your honor to others
  and your dignity[a] to one who is cruel,
¹⁰lest strangers feast on your wealth
  and your toil enrich the house of another.
¹¹At the end of your life you will groan,
  when your flesh and body are spent.
¹²You will say, "How I hated discipline!
  How my heart spurned correction!
¹³I would not obey my teachers
  or turn my ear to my instructors.

---

[a] 9 Or *years*

¹⁴And I was soon in serious trouble
  in the assembly of God's people."

¹⁵Drink water from your own cistern,
  running water from your own well.
¹⁶Should your springs overflow in the streets,
  your streams of water in the public squares?
¹⁷Let them be yours alone,
  never to be shared with strangers.
¹⁸May your fountain be blessed,
  and may you rejoice in the wife of your youth.
¹⁹A loving doe, a graceful deer —
  may her breasts satisfy you always,
  may you ever be intoxicated with her love.
²⁰Why, my son, be intoxicated with another man's wife?
  Why embrace the bosom of a wayward woman?

²¹For your ways are in full view of the Lord,
  and he examines all your paths.
²²The evil deeds of the wicked ensnare them;
  the cords of their sins hold them fast.
²³For lack of discipline they will die,
  led astray by their own great folly.

Warnings Against Folly

6 My son, if you have put up security for your neighbor,
  if you have shaken hands in pledge for a stranger,
²you have been trapped by what you said,
  ensnared by the words of your mouth.
³So do this, my son, to free yourself,
  since you have fallen into your neighbor's hands:

Go — to the point of exhaustion — [a]
and give your neighbor no rest!
[4] Allow no sleep to your eyes,
no slumber to your eyelids.
[5] Free yourself, like a gazelle from the hand
of the hunter,
like a bird from the snare of the fowler.

[6] Go to the ant, you sluggard;
consider its ways and be wise!
[7] It has no commander,
no overseer or ruler,
[8] yet it stores its provisions in summer
and gathers its food at harvest.

[9] How long will you lie there, you sluggard?
When will you get up from your sleep?
[10] A little sleep, a little slumber,
a little folding of the hands to rest —
[11] and poverty will come on you like a thief
and scarcity like an armed man.

[12] A troublemaker and a villain,
who goes about with a corrupt mouth,
[13] who winks maliciously with his eye,
signals with his feet
and motions with his fingers,
[14] who plots evil with deceit in his heart —
he always stirs up conflict.
[15] Therefore disaster will overtake him in an instant;
he will suddenly be destroyed — without remedy.

---

[a] 3 Or *Go and humble yourself,*

¹⁶There are six things the LORD hates,
  seven that are detestable to him:
¹⁷ haughty eyes,
  a lying tongue,
  hands that shed innocent blood,
¹⁸ a heart that devises wicked schemes,
  feet that are quick to rush into evil,
¹⁹ a false witness who pours out lies
  and a person who stirs up conflict in the community.

Warning Against Adultery

²⁰My son, keep your father's command
  and do not forsake your mother's teaching.
²¹Bind them always on your heart;
  fasten them around your neck.
²²When you walk, they will guide you;
  when you sleep, they will watch over you;
  when you awake, they will speak to you.
²³For this command is a lamp,
  this teaching is a light,
  and correction and instruction
  are the way to life,
²⁴keeping you from your neighbor's wife,
  from the smooth talk of a wayward woman.

²⁵Do not lust in your heart after her beauty
  or let her captivate you with her eyes.
²⁶For a prostitute can be had for a loaf of bread,
  but another man's wife preys on your very life.
²⁷Can a man scoop fire into his lap
  without his clothes being burned?

²⁸Can a man walk on hot coals
   without his feet being scorched?
²⁹So is he who sleeps with another man's wife;
   no one who touches her will go unpunished.

³⁰People do not despise a thief if he steals
   to satisfy his hunger when he is starving.
³¹Yet if he is caught, he must pay sevenfold,
   though it costs him all the wealth of his house.
³²But a man who commits adultery has no sense;
   whoever does so destroys himself.
³³Blows and disgrace are his lot,
   and his shame will never be wiped away.

³⁴For jealousy arouses a husband's fury,
   and he will show no mercy when he takes revenge.
³⁵He will not accept any compensation;
   he will refuse a bribe, however great it is.

Warning Against the Adulterous Woman

7 My son, keep my words
   and store up my commands within you.
²Keep my commands and you will live;
   guard my teachings as the apple of your eye.
³Bind them on your fingers;
   write them on the tablet of your heart.
⁴Say to wisdom, "You are my sister,"
   and to insight, "You are my relative."
⁵They will keep you from the adulterous woman,
   from the wayward woman with her seductive words.

⁶At the window of my house
   I looked down through the lattice.

⁷I saw among the simple,
  I noticed among the young men,
  a youth who had no sense.
⁸He was going down the street near her corner,
  walking along in the direction of her house
⁹at twilight, as the day was fading,
  as the dark of night set in.

¹⁰Then out came a woman to meet him,
  dressed like a prostitute and with crafty intent.
¹¹(She is unruly and defiant,
  her feet never stay at home;
¹²now in the street, now in the squares,
  at every corner she lurks.)
¹³She took hold of him and kissed him
  and with a brazen face she said:

¹⁴"Today I fulfilled my vows,
  and I have food from my fellowship offering at home.
¹⁵So I came out to meet you;
  I looked for you and have found you!
¹⁶I have covered my bed
  with colored linens from Egypt.
¹⁷I have perfumed my bed
  with myrrh, aloes and cinnamon.
¹⁸Come, let's drink deeply of love till morning;
  let's enjoy ourselves with love!
¹⁹My husband is not at home;
  he has gone on a long journey.
²⁰He took his purse filled with money
  and will not be home till full moon."

²¹With persuasive words she led him astray;
    she seduced him with her smooth talk.
²²All at once he followed her
    like an ox going to the slaughter,
  like a deer[a] stepping into a noose[b]
²³   till an arrow pierces his liver,
  like a bird darting into a snare,
    little knowing it will cost him his life.

²⁴Now then, my sons, listen to me;
    pay attention to what I say.
²⁵Do not let your heart turn to her ways
    or stray into her paths.
²⁶Many are the victims she has brought down;
    her slain are a mighty throng.
²⁷Her house is a highway to the grave,
    leading down to the chambers of death.

Wisdom's Call

8 Does not wisdom call out?
  Does not understanding raise her voice?
²At the highest point along the way,
    where the paths meet, she takes her stand;
³beside the gate leading into the city,
    at the entrance, she cries aloud:
⁴"To you, O people, I call out;
    I raise my voice to all mankind.
⁵You who are simple, gain prudence;
    you who are foolish, set your hearts on it.[c]

---

[a] 22 Syriac (see also Septuagint); Hebrew *fool*   [b] 22 The meaning of the Hebrew for this line is uncertain.   [c] 5 Septuagint; Hebrew *foolish, instruct your minds*

⁶Listen, for I have trustworthy things to say;
  I open my lips to speak what is right.
⁷My mouth speaks what is true,
  for my lips detest wickedness.
⁸All the words of my mouth are just;
  none of them is crooked or perverse.
⁹To the discerning all of them are right;
  they are upright to those who have found knowledge.
¹⁰Choose my instruction instead of silver,
  knowledge rather than choice gold,
¹¹for wisdom is more precious than rubies,
  and nothing you desire can compare with her.

¹²"I, wisdom, dwell together with prudence;
  I possess knowledge and discretion.
¹³To fear the LORD is to hate evil;
  I hate pride and arrogance,
  evil behavior and perverse speech.
¹⁴Counsel and sound judgment are mine;
  I have insight, I have power.
¹⁵By me kings reign
  and rulers issue decrees that are just;
¹⁶by me princes govern,
  and nobles — all who rule on earth.[a]
¹⁷I love those who love me,
  and those who seek me find me.
¹⁸With me are riches and honor,
  enduring wealth and prosperity.
¹⁹My fruit is better than fine gold;
  what I yield surpasses choice silver.

---

[a] 16 Some Hebrew manuscripts and Septuagint; other Hebrew manuscripts *all righteous rulers*

Arrogance and Pride

To fear the LORD is to hate evil; I hate pride and arrogance,
evil behavior and perverse speech.
PROVERBS 8:13

In *The Screwtape Letters* written by C. S. Lewis, a senior devil urges his young protégé to divert a Christian's thoughts away from God and focus instead on the faults of the people around him at church.

During a Sunday service, I found myself distracted and somewhat annoyed by a person near me. He sang loudly off key and was out of sync during the unison readings. But when we bowed our heads for a time of silent prayer, it struck me that the Lord must surely be more pleased with that other person's heart than with the judgmental feelings He saw in mine.

A few days later I happened to read Proverbs 8 and was struck by verse 13 where wisdom personified declares, "I hate pride and arrogance, evil behavior and perverse speech." Throughout this chapter, wisdom calls to us to gain a prudent or understanding heart (v. 5) and to find life and obtain favor from the Lord (v. 35). The alternative is to go through life with a superior attitude while dying inside in the process (v. 36).

Pride is a sword that wounds the person who uses it along with those against whom it is used. Arrogance robs us of all God longs to give us, but "humility is the fear of the LORD; its wages are riches and honor and life" (22:4).

—DAVID McCASLAND

Pride brings shame. Humility brings wisdom.

²⁰I walk in the way of righteousness,
　　along the paths of justice,
²¹bestowing a rich inheritance on those who love me
　　and making their treasuries full.

²²"The Lord brought me forth as the first of his works,[a,b]
　　before his deeds of old;
²³I was formed long ages ago,
　　at the very beginning, when the world came to be.
²⁴When there were no watery depths, I was given birth,
　　when there were no springs overflowing with water;
²⁵before the mountains were settled in place,
　　before the hills, I was given birth,
²⁶before he made the world or its fields
　　or any of the dust of the earth.
²⁷I was there when he set the heavens in place,
　　when he marked out the horizon on the face of the
　　　　deep,
²⁸when he established the clouds above
　　and fixed securely the fountains of the deep,
²⁹when he gave the sea its boundary
　　so the waters would not overstep his command,
　　and when he marked out the foundations of the earth.
³⁰　Then I was constantly[c] at his side.
　I was filled with delight day after day,
　　rejoicing always in his presence,
³¹rejoicing in his whole world
　　and delighting in mankind.

---

[a] 22 Or *way*; or *dominion*　　[b] 22 Or *The Lord possessed me at the beginning of his work*; or *The Lord brought me forth at the beginning of his work*　　[c] 30 Or *was the artisan*; or *was a little child*

[32] "Now then, my children, listen to me;
　　blessed are those who keep my ways.
[33] Listen to my instruction and be wise;
　　do not disregard it.
[34] Blessed are those who listen to me,
　　watching daily at my doors,
　　waiting at my doorway.
[35] For those who find me find life
　　and receive favor from the Lord.
[36] But those who fail to find me harm themselves;
　　all who hate me love death."

Invitations of Wisdom and Folly

9 Wisdom has built her house;
　　she has set up[a] its seven pillars.
[2] She has prepared her meat and mixed her wine;
　　she has also set her table.
[3] She has sent out her servants, and she calls
　　from the highest point of the city,
[4] 　"Let all who are simple come to my house!"
　To those who have no sense she says,
[5] 　"Come, eat my food
　　and drink the wine I have mixed.
[6] Leave your simple ways and you will live;
　　walk in the way of insight."

[7] Whoever corrects a mocker invites insults;
　　whoever rebukes the wicked incurs abuse.
[8] Do not rebuke mockers or they will hate you;
　　rebuke the wise and they will love you.

---

[a] 1 Septuagint, Syriac and Targum; Hebrew *has hewn out*

⁹Instruct the wise and they will be wiser still;
  teach the righteous and they will add to their learning.

¹⁰The fear of the Lᴏʀᴅ is the beginning of wisdom,
  and knowledge of the Holy One is understanding.
¹¹For through wisdom*a* your days will be many,
  and years will be added to your life.
¹²If you are wise, your wisdom will reward you;
  if you are a mocker, you alone will suffer.

¹³Folly is an unruly woman;
  she is simple and knows nothing.
¹⁴She sits at the door of her house,
  on a seat at the highest point of the city,
¹⁵calling out to those who pass by,
  who go straight on their way,
¹⁶ "Let all who are simple come to my house!"
To those who have no sense she says,
¹⁷ "Stolen water is sweet;
  food eaten in secret is delicious!"
¹⁸But little do they know that the dead are there,
  that her guests are deep in the realm of the dead.

Proverbs of Solomon

10 The proverbs of Solomon:

A wise son brings joy to his father,
  but a foolish son brings grief to his mother.
²Ill-gotten treasures have no lasting value,
  but righteousness delivers from death.

---

a 11 Septuagint, Syriac and Targum; Hebrew *me*

³The LORD does not let the righteous go hungry,
  but he thwarts the craving of the wicked.

⁴Lazy hands make for poverty,
  but diligent hands bring wealth.

⁵He who gathers crops in summer is a prudent son,
  but he who sleeps during harvest is a disgraceful son.

⁶Blessings crown the head of the righteous,
  but violence overwhelms the mouth of the wicked.ᵃ

⁷The name of the righteous is used in blessings,ᵇ
  but the name of the wicked will rot.

⁸The wise in heart accept commands,
  but a chattering fool comes to ruin.

⁹Whoever walks in integrity walks securely,
  but whoever takes crooked paths will be found out.

¹⁰Whoever winks maliciously causes grief,
  and a chattering fool comes to ruin.

¹¹The mouth of the righteous is a fountain of life,
  but the mouth of the wicked conceals violence.

¹²Hatred stirs up conflict,
  but love covers over all wrongs.

¹³Wisdom is found on the lips of the discerning,
  but a rod is for the back of one who has no sense.

¹⁴The wise store up knowledge,
  but the mouth of a fool invites ruin.

¹⁵The wealth of the rich is their fortified city,
  but poverty is the ruin of the poor.

ᵃ 6 Or *righteous, / but the mouth of the wicked conceals violence*   ᵇ 7 See Gen. 48:20.

¹⁶The wages of the righteous is life,
  but the earnings of the wicked are sin and death.

¹⁷Whoever heeds discipline shows the way to life,
  but whoever ignores correction leads others astray.

¹⁸Whoever conceals hatred with lying lips
  and spreads slander is a fool.

¹⁹Sin is not ended by multiplying words,
  but the prudent hold their tongues.

²⁰The tongue of the righteous is choice silver,
  but the heart of the wicked is of little value.

²¹The lips of the righteous nourish many,
  but fools die for lack of sense.

²²The blessing of the LORD brings wealth,
  without painful toil for it.

²³A fool finds pleasure in wicked schemes,
  but a person of understanding delights in wisdom.

²⁴What the wicked dread will overtake them;
  what the righteous desire will be granted.

²⁵When the storm has swept by, the wicked are gone,
  but the righteous stand firm forever.

²⁶As vinegar to the teeth and smoke to the eyes,
  so are sluggards to those who send them.

²⁷The fear of the LORD adds length to life,
  but the years of the wicked are cut short.

²⁸The prospect of the righteous is joy,
  but the hopes of the wicked come to nothing.

²⁹The way of the LORD is a refuge for the blameless,
but it is the ruin of those who do evil.

³⁰The righteous will never be uprooted,
but the wicked will not remain in the land.

³¹From the mouth of the righteous comes the fruit of
wisdom,
but a perverse tongue will be silenced.

³²The lips of the righteous know what finds favor,
but the mouth of the wicked only what is perverse.

11 The LORD detests dishonest scales,
but accurate weights find favor with him.

²When pride comes, then comes disgrace,
but with humility comes wisdom.

³The integrity of the upright guides them,
but the unfaithful are destroyed by their duplicity.

⁴Wealth is worthless in the day of wrath,
but righteousness delivers from death.

⁵The righteousness of the blameless makes their paths
straight,
but the wicked are brought down by their own
wickedness.

⁶The righteousness of the upright delivers them,
but the unfaithful are trapped by evil desires.

⁷Hopes placed in mortals die with them;
all the promise ofᵃ their power comes to nothing.

ᵃ 7 Two Hebrew manuscripts; most Hebrew manuscripts, Vulgate, Syriac and
Targum *When the wicked die, their hope perishes; / all they expected from*

⁸The righteous person is rescued from trouble,
and it falls on the wicked instead.

⁹With their mouths the godless destroy their neighbors,
but through knowledge the righteous escape.

¹⁰When the righteous prosper, the city rejoices;
when the wicked perish, there are shouts of joy.

¹¹Through the blessing of the upright a city is exalted,
but by the mouth of the wicked it is destroyed.

¹²Whoever derides their neighbor has no sense,
but the one who has understanding holds their tongue.

¹³A gossip betrays a confidence,
but a trustworthy person keeps a secret.

¹⁴For lack of guidance a nation falls,
but victory is won through many advisers.

¹⁵Whoever puts up security for a stranger will surely
suffer,
but whoever refuses to shake hands in pledge is safe.

¹⁶A kindhearted woman gains honor,
but ruthless men gain only wealth.

¹⁷Those who are kind benefit themselves,
but the cruel bring ruin on themselves.

¹⁸A wicked person earns deceptive wages,
but the one who sows righteousness reaps a sure
reward.

¹⁹Truly the righteous attain life,
but whoever pursues evil finds death.

²⁰The LORD detests those whose hearts are perverse,
  but he delights in those whose ways are blameless.

²¹Be sure of this: The wicked will not go unpunished,
  but those who are righteous will go free.

²²Like a gold ring in a pig's snout
  is a beautiful woman who shows no discretion.

²³The desire of the righteous ends only in good,
  but the hope of the wicked only in wrath.

²⁴One person gives freely, yet gains even more;
  another withholds unduly, but comes to poverty.

²⁵A generous person will prosper;
  whoever refreshes others will be refreshed.

²⁶People curse the one who hoards grain,
  but they pray God's blessing on the one who is willing
    to sell.

²⁷Whoever seeks good finds favor,
  but evil comes to one who searches for it.

²⁸Those who trust in their riches will fall,
  but the righteous will thrive like a green leaf.

²⁹Whoever brings ruin on their family will inherit only
    wind,
  and the fool will be servant to the wise.

³⁰The fruit of the righteous is a tree of life,
  and the one who is wise saves lives.

³¹If the righteous receive their due on earth,
  how much more the ungodly and the sinner!

12 Whoever loves discipline loves knowledge,
but whoever hates correction is stupid.

²Good people obtain favor from the LORD,
but he condemns those who devise wicked schemes.

³No one can be established through wickedness,
but the righteous cannot be uprooted.

⁴A wife of noble character is her husband's crown,
but a disgraceful wife is like decay in his bones.

⁵The plans of the righteous are just,
but the advice of the wicked is deceitful.

⁶The words of the wicked lie in wait for blood,
but the speech of the upright rescues them.

⁷The wicked are overthrown and are no more,
but the house of the righteous stands firm.

⁸A person is praised according to their prudence,
and one with a warped mind is despised.

⁹Better to be a nobody and yet have a servant
than pretend to be somebody and have no food.

¹⁰The righteous care for the needs of their animals,
but the kindest acts of the wicked are cruel.

¹¹Those who work their land will have abundant food,
but those who chase fantasies have no sense.

¹²The wicked desire the stronghold of evildoers,
but the root of the righteous endures.

¹³Evildoers are trapped by their sinful talk,
and so the innocent escape trouble.

[14]From the fruit of their lips people are filled with good
     things,
  and the work of their hands brings them reward.

[15]The way of fools seems right to them,
  but the wise listen to advice.

[16]Fools show their annoyance at once,
  but the prudent overlook an insult.

[17]An honest witness tells the truth,
  but a false witness tells lies.

[18]The words of the reckless pierce like swords,
  but the tongue of the wise brings healing.

[19]Truthful lips endure forever,
  but a lying tongue lasts only a moment.

[20]Deceit is in the hearts of those who plot evil,
  but those who promote peace have joy.

[21]No harm overtakes the righteous,
  but the wicked have their fill of trouble.

[22]The LORD detests lying lips,
  but he delights in people who are trustworthy.

[23]The prudent keep their knowledge to themselves,
  but a fool's heart blurts out folly.

[24]Diligent hands will rule,
  but laziness ends in forced labor.

[25]Anxiety weighs down the heart,
  but a kind word cheers it up.

[26]The righteous choose their friends carefully,
  but the way of the wicked leads them astray.

²⁷The lazy do not roast*ᵃ* any game,
  but the diligent feed on the riches of the hunt.

²⁸In the way of righteousness there is life;
  along that path is immortality.

13 A wise son heeds his father's instruction,
  but a mocker does not respond to rebukes.

²From the fruit of their lips people enjoy good things,
  but the unfaithful have an appetite for violence.

³Those who guard their lips preserve their lives,
  but those who speak rashly will come to ruin.

⁴A sluggard's appetite is never filled,
  but the desires of the diligent are fully satisfied.

⁵The righteous hate what is false,
  but the wicked make themselves a stench
  and bring shame on themselves.

⁶Righteousness guards the person of integrity,
  but wickedness overthrows the sinner.

⁷One person pretends to be rich, yet has nothing;
  another pretends to be poor, yet has great wealth.

⁸A person's riches may ransom their life,
  but the poor cannot respond to threatening rebukes.

⁹The light of the righteous shines brightly,
  but the lamp of the wicked is snuffed out.

¹⁰Where there is strife, there is pride,
  but wisdom is found in those who take advice.

¹¹Dishonest money dwindles away,
  but whoever gathers money little by little makes it grow.

ᵃ 27 The meaning of the Hebrew for this word is uncertain.

The Two Bears

Where there is strife, there is pride,
but wisdom is found in those who take advice.
PROVERBS 13:10

Some years ago, my wife, Carolyn, and I spent a few days camping on the flanks of Mount Rainier in Washington State. When we were returning to our campsite one evening, we saw in the middle of a meadow two male bears boxing each other's ears. We stopped to watch.

There was a hiker nearby, and I asked him what the conflict was about. "A young female," he said.

"Where is she?" I asked.

"Oh, she left about twenty minutes ago," he chuckled. Thus, I gathered, the conflict at this point was not about the female bear but about being the toughest bear.

Most fights aren't about policy and principle, or about right and wrong; they're almost always about pride. The wise man of Proverbs swings his axe at the root of the problem when he writes: "Where there is strife, there is pride" (13:10). Quarrels are fueled by pride, by needing to be right, by wanting our way, or by defending our turf or our egos.

On the other side, wisdom resides with the well-advised—those who listen and learn. There is wisdom in all who humble themselves—who set aside selfish ambition, acknowledge the limits of their understanding, and listen to others' points of view.

This is the wisdom from God, and it spreads peace wherever it goes.

—DAVID ROPER

Humility brings wisdom.

[12]Hope deferred makes the heart sick,
  but a longing fulfilled is a tree of life.

[13]Whoever scorns instruction will pay for it,
  but whoever respects a command is rewarded.

[14]The teaching of the wise is a fountain of life,
  turning a person from the snares of death.

[15]Good judgment wins favor,
  but the way of the unfaithful leads to their destruction.[a]

[16]All who are prudent act with[b] knowledge,
  but fools expose their folly.

[17]A wicked messenger falls into trouble,
  but a trustworthy envoy brings healing.

[18]Whoever disregards discipline comes to poverty and
    shame,
  but whoever heeds correction is honored.

[19]A longing fulfilled is sweet to the soul,
  but fools detest turning from evil.

[20]Walk with the wise and become wise,
  for a companion of fools suffers harm.

[21]Trouble pursues the sinner,
  but the righteous are rewarded with good things.

[22]A good person leaves an inheritance for their children's
    children,
  but a sinner's wealth is stored up for the righteous.

[23]An unplowed field produces food for the poor,
  but injustice sweeps it away.

---

[a] 15 Septuagint and Syriac; the meaning of the Hebrew for this phrase is
uncertain.   [b] 16 Or *prudent protect themselves through*

²⁴Whoever spares the rod hates their children,
  but the one who loves their children is careful to
    discipline them.

²⁵The righteous eat to their hearts' content,
  but the stomach of the wicked goes hungry.

14 The wise woman builds her house,
    but with her own hands the foolish one tears hers
    down.

²Whoever fears the LORD walks uprightly,
  but those who despise him are devious in their ways.

³A fool's mouth lashes out with pride,
  but the lips of the wise protect them.

⁴Where there are no oxen, the manger is empty,
  but from the strength of an ox come abundant
    harvests.

⁵An honest witness does not deceive,
  but a false witness pours out lies.

⁶The mocker seeks wisdom and finds none,
  but knowledge comes easily to the discerning.

⁷Stay away from a fool,
  for you will not find knowledge on their lips.

⁸The wisdom of the prudent is to give thought to their
    ways,
  but the folly of fools is deception.

⁹Fools mock at making amends for sin,
  but goodwill is found among the upright.

¹⁰Each heart knows its own bitterness,
  and no one else can share its joy.

¹¹The house of the wicked will be destroyed,
    but the tent of the upright will flourish.

¹²There is a way that appears to be right,
    but in the end it leads to death.

¹³Even in laughter the heart may ache,
    and rejoicing may end in grief.

¹⁴The faithless will be fully repaid for their ways,
    and the good rewarded for theirs.

¹⁵The simple believe anything,
    but the prudent give thought to their steps.

¹⁶The wise fear the Lord and shun evil,
    but a fool is hotheaded and yet feels secure.

¹⁷A quick-tempered person does foolish things,
    and the one who devises evil schemes is hated.

¹⁸The simple inherit folly,
    but the prudent are crowned with knowledge.

¹⁹Evildoers will bow down in the presence of the good,
    and the wicked at the gates of the righteous.

²⁰The poor are shunned even by their neighbors,
    but the rich have many friends.

²¹It is a sin to despise one's neighbor,
    but blessed is the one who is kind to the needy.

²²Do not those who plot evil go astray?
    But those who plan what is good find^{*a*} love and
        faithfulness.

²³All hard work brings a profit,
    but mere talk leads only to poverty.

---

[a] 22 Or *show*

²⁴The wealth of the wise is their crown,
    but the folly of fools yields folly.

²⁵A truthful witness saves lives,
    but a false witness is deceitful.

²⁶Whoever fears the LORD has a secure fortress,
    and for their children it will be a refuge.

²⁷The fear of the LORD is a fountain of life,
    turning a person from the snares of death.

²⁸A large population is a king's glory,
    but without subjects a prince is ruined.

²⁹Whoever is patient has great understanding,
    but one who is quick-tempered displays folly.

³⁰A heart at peace gives life to the body,
    but envy rots the bones.

³¹Whoever oppresses the poor shows contempt for their
    Maker,
    but whoever is kind to the needy honors God.

³²When calamity comes, the wicked are brought down,
    but even in death the righteous seek refuge in God.

³³Wisdom reposes in the heart of the discerning
    and even among fools she lets herself be known.ᵃ

³⁴Righteousness exalts a nation,
    but sin condemns any people.

³⁵A king delights in a wise servant,
    but a shameful servant arouses his fury.

ᵃ 33 Hebrew; Septuagint and Syriac *discerning / but in the heart of fools she is not known*

Boston Gentle

A gentle answer turns away wrath, but a harsh word stirs up anger.
PROVERBS 15:1

My car broke down in a tunnel during rush hour in downtown Boston. Angry drivers expressed their frustration as they struggled past me. Eventually, the car was towed to a station for repairs. Later it broke down again, stranding me along the Interstate at 2 a.m. Back to the shop it went.

Unfortunately, the repair shop also doubled as a parking lot during Red Sox baseball games. When I arrived after work the next day to pick up my car, it was hemmed in by thirty other vehicles!

Let's just say I was less than Christlike in my initial reaction. I ranted and raved, and then, realizing it was only making them less willing to help me at the close of their day, I decided to give up. I stormed toward the glass doors and struggled to get them open. My anger increased when the station workers laughed at me.

I had barely made it out when I realized how unlike Christ I'd been. Chastened, I rapped on the locked doors and mouthed, "I'm sorry" to the staff inside. They were stunned! They let me back in, and I meekly told them that Christians shouldn't behave as I had. Minutes later, they were shifting cars to free up mine. I learned the truth that soft rather than harsh words can change circumstances (Proverbs 15:1).

—RANDY KILGORE

A soft answer has often been the means of breaking a hard heart.

15

A gentle answer turns away wrath,
but a harsh word stirs up anger.
2 The tongue of the wise adorns knowledge,
but the mouth of the fool gushes folly.
3 The eyes of the LORD are everywhere,
keeping watch on the wicked and the good.
4 The soothing tongue is a tree of life,
but a perverse tongue crushes the spirit.
5 A fool spurns a parent's discipline,
but whoever heeds correction shows prudence.
6 The house of the righteous contains great treasure,
but the income of the wicked brings ruin.
7 The lips of the wise spread knowledge,
but the hearts of fools are not upright.
8 The LORD detests the sacrifice of the wicked,
but the prayer of the upright pleases him.
9 The LORD detests the way of the wicked,
but he loves those who pursue righteousness.
10 Stern discipline awaits anyone who leaves the path;
the one who hates correction will die.
11 Death and Destruction[a] lie open before the LORD —
how much more do human hearts!
12 Mockers resent correction,
so they avoid the wise.
13 A happy heart makes the face cheerful,
but heartache crushes the spirit.

---

[a] 11 Hebrew *Abaddon*

¹⁴The discerning heart seeks knowledge,
  but the mouth of a fool feeds on folly.

¹⁵All the days of the oppressed are wretched,
  but the cheerful heart has a continual feast.

¹⁶Better a little with the fear of the LORD
  than great wealth with turmoil.

¹⁷Better a small serving of vegetables with love
  than a fattened calf with hatred.

¹⁸A hot-tempered person stirs up conflict,
  but the one who is patient calms a quarrel.

¹⁹The way of the sluggard is blocked with thorns,
  but the path of the upright is a highway.

²⁰A wise son brings joy to his father,
  but a foolish man despises his mother.

²¹Folly brings joy to one who has no sense,
  but whoever has understanding keeps a straight
    course.

²²Plans fail for lack of counsel,
  but with many advisers they succeed.

²³A person finds joy in giving an apt reply—
  and how good is a timely word!

²⁴The path of life leads upward for the prudent
  to keep them from going down to the realm of the
    dead.

²⁵The LORD tears down the house of the proud,
  but he sets the widow's boundary stones in place.

²⁶The LORD detests the thoughts of the wicked,
  but gracious words are pure in his sight.

²⁷The greedy bring ruin to their households,
  but the one who hates bribes will live.

²⁸The heart of the righteous weighs its answers,
  but the mouth of the wicked gushes evil.

²⁹The LORD is far from the wicked,
  but he hears the prayer of the righteous.

³⁰Light in a messenger's eyes brings joy to the heart,
  and good news gives health to the bones.

³¹Whoever heeds life-giving correction
  will be at home among the wise.

³²Those who disregard discipline despise themselves,
  but the one who heeds correction gains
    understanding.

³³Wisdom's instruction is to fear the LORD,
  and humility comes before honor.

16 To humans belong the plans of the heart,
  but from the LORD comes the proper answer of the
    tongue.

²All a person's ways seem pure to them,
  but motives are weighed by the LORD.

³Commit to the LORD whatever you do,
  and he will establish your plans.

⁴The LORD works out everything to its proper end —
  even the wicked for a day of disaster.

⁵The LORD detests all the proud of heart.
  Be sure of this: They will not go unpunished.

⁶Through love and faithfulness sin is atoned for;
  through the fear of the LORD evil is avoided.

⁷When the Lord takes pleasure in anyone's way,
  he causes their enemies to make peace with them.

⁸Better a little with righteousness
  than much gain with injustice.

⁹In their hearts humans plan their course,
  but the Lord establishes their steps.

¹⁰The lips of a king speak as an oracle,
  and his mouth does not betray justice.

¹¹Honest scales and balances belong to the Lord;
  all the weights in the bag are of his making.

¹²Kings detest wrongdoing,
  for a throne is established through righteousness.

¹³Kings take pleasure in honest lips;
  they value the one who speaks what is right.

¹⁴A king's wrath is a messenger of death,
  but the wise will appease it.

¹⁵When a king's face brightens, it means life;
  his favor is like a rain cloud in spring.

¹⁶How much better to get wisdom than gold,
  to get insight rather than silver!

¹⁷The highway of the upright avoids evil;
  those who guard their ways preserve their lives.

¹⁸Pride goes before destruction,
  a haughty spirit before a fall.

¹⁹Better to be lowly in spirit along with the oppressed
  than to share plunder with the proud.

Right Place

In their hearts humans plan their course,
but the LORD establishes their steps.
PROVERBS 16:9

They were in the right place but on the wrong day. Or so it would seem.

A traveling high school singing group arrived at a nursing home for a Thursday concert. However, the folks at the home were expecting them on Friday. But they said if the group could get set up fast, they could sing for twenty minutes. Then they'd have to stop for a memorial service for one of the residents.

The chorale hurriedly got ready and sang, and as they did, the son of the man who had died heard them. When they were done, he asked if they could sing at his dad's service. The teens gladly agreed, and they were able to minister hope and truth to all who attended. God used these young people in a special way—all because of a secretarial error. But was it a mistake?

We carefully make schedules so we can be where we think we should be. But we always need to keep in mind the words of Solomon, "In their hearts humans plan their course, but the LORD establishes their steps." (Proverbs 16:9).

Do we seek ministry in life's unplanned schedule changes? Do we turn detours into guided tours of what He wants to do through us? If we're doing God's will, we'll be in the right place. Then, wherever we are, we can point people to Him.

—DAVE BRANON

Unexpected changes are opportunities in disguise.

²⁰Whoever gives heed to instruction prospers,ᵃ
and blessed is the one who trusts in the LORD.

²¹The wise in heart are called discerning,
and gracious words promote instruction.ᵇ

²²Prudence is a fountain of life to the prudent,
but folly brings punishment to fools.

²³The hearts of the wise make their mouths prudent,
and their lips promote instruction.ᶜ

²⁴Gracious words are a honeycomb,
sweet to the soul and healing to the bones.

²⁵There is a way that appears to be right,
but in the end it leads to death.

²⁶The appetite of laborers works for them;
their hunger drives them on.

²⁷A scoundrel plots evil,
and on their lips it is like a scorching fire.

²⁸A perverse person stirs up conflict,
and a gossip separates close friends.

²⁹A violent person entices their neighbor
and leads them down a path that is not good.

³⁰Whoever winks with their eye is plotting perversity;
whoever purses their lips is bent on evil.

³¹Gray hair is a crown of splendor;
it is attained in the way of righteousness.

³²Better a patient person than a warrior,
one with self-control than one who takes a city.

ᵃ 20 Or *whoever speaks prudently finds what is good*   ᵇ 21 Or *words make a person persuasive*   ᶜ 23 Or *prudent / and make their lips persuasive*

³³The lot is cast into the lap,
    but its every decision is from the LORD.

17 Better a dry crust with peace and quiet
    than a house full of feasting, with strife.

²A prudent servant will rule over a disgraceful son
    and will share the inheritance as one of the family.

³The crucible for silver and the furnace for gold,
    but the LORD tests the heart.

⁴A wicked person listens to deceitful lips;
    a liar pays attention to a destructive tongue.

⁵Whoever mocks the poor shows contempt for their
    Maker;
    whoever gloats over disaster will not go unpunished.

⁶Children's children are a crown to the aged,
    and parents are the pride of their children.

⁷Eloquent lips are unsuited to a godless fool —
    how much worse lying lips to a ruler!

⁸A bribe is seen as a charm by the one who gives it;
    they think success will come at every turn.

⁹Whoever would foster love covers over an offense,
    but whoever repeats the matter separates close friends.

¹⁰A rebuke impresses a discerning person
    more than a hundred lashes a fool.

¹¹Evildoers foster rebellion against God;
    the messenger of death will be sent against them.

¹²Better to meet a bear robbed of her cubs
    than a fool bent on folly.

¹³Evil will never leave the house
   of one who pays back evil for good.

¹⁴Starting a quarrel is like breaching a dam;
   so drop the matter before a dispute breaks out.

¹⁵Acquitting the guilty and condemning the innocent —
   the Lord detests them both.

¹⁶Why should fools have money in hand to buy wisdom,
   when they are not able to understand it?

¹⁷A friend loves at all times,
   and a brother is born for a time of adversity.

¹⁸One who has no sense shakes hands in pledge
   and puts up security for a neighbor.

¹⁹Whoever loves a quarrel loves sin;
   whoever builds a high gate invites destruction.

²⁰One whose heart is corrupt does not prosper;
   one whose tongue is perverse falls into trouble.

²¹To have a fool for a child brings grief;
   there is no joy for the parent of a godless fool.

²²A cheerful heart is good medicine,
   but a crushed spirit dries up the bones.

²³The wicked accept bribes in secret
   to pervert the course of justice.

²⁴A discerning person keeps wisdom in view,
   but a fool's eyes wander to the ends of the earth.

²⁵A foolish son brings grief to his father
   and bitterness to the mother who bore him.

²⁶If imposing a fine on the innocent is not good,
   surely to flog honest officials is not right.

²⁷The one who has knowledge uses words with restraint,
and whoever has understanding is even-tempered.

²⁸Even fools are thought wise if they keep silent,
and discerning if they hold their tongues.

18 An unfriendly person pursues selfish ends
and against all sound judgment starts quarrels.

²Fools find no pleasure in understanding
but delight in airing their own opinions.

³When wickedness comes, so does contempt,
and with shame comes reproach.

⁴The words of the mouth are deep waters,
but the fountain of wisdom is a rushing stream.

⁵It is not good to be partial to the wicked
and so deprive the innocent of justice.

⁶The lips of fools bring them strife,
and their mouths invite a beating.

⁷The mouths of fools are their undoing,
and their lips are a snare to their very lives.

⁸The words of a gossip are like choice morsels;
they go down to the inmost parts.

⁹One who is slack in his work
is brother to one who destroys.

¹⁰The name of the LORD is a fortified tower;
the righteous run to it and are safe.

¹¹The wealth of the rich is their fortified city;
they imagine it a wall too high to scale.

¹²Before a downfall the heart is haughty,
but humility comes before honor.

¹³To answer before listening —
that is folly and shame.

¹⁴The human spirit can endure in sickness,
but a crushed spirit who can bear?

¹⁵The heart of the discerning acquires knowledge,
for the ears of the wise seek it out.

¹⁶A gift opens the way
and ushers the giver into the presence of the great.

¹⁷In a lawsuit the first to speak seems right,
until someone comes forward and cross-examines.

¹⁸Casting the lot settles disputes
and keeps strong opponents apart.

¹⁹A brother wronged is more unyielding than a fortified
city;
disputes are like the barred gates of a citadel.

²⁰From the fruit of their mouth a person's stomach is filled;
with the harvest of their lips they are satisfied.

²¹The tongue has the power of life and death,
and those who love it will eat its fruit.

²²He who finds a wife finds what is good
and receives favor from the LORD.

²³The poor plead for mercy,
but the rich answer harshly.

²⁴One who has unreliable friends soon comes to ruin,
but there is a friend who sticks closer than a brother.

19 Better the poor whose walk is blameless
than a fool whose lips are perverse.

The Power of Words

*The tongue has the power of life and death,
and those who love it will eat its fruit.*
PROVERBS 18:21

Nelson Mandela, who opposed the South African apartheid regime and was imprisoned for almost three decades, knew the power of words. He is often quoted today, but while in prison his words could not be quoted for fear of repercussion. A decade after his release he said: "It is never my custom to use words lightly. If twenty-seven years in prison have done anything to us, it was to use the silence of solitude to make us understand how precious words are, and how real speech is in its impact on the way people live and die."

King Solomon, author of most of the Old Testament book of Proverbs, wrote often about the power of words. He said, "The tongue has the power of life and death" (18:21). Words have the potential to produce positive or negative consequences (v. 20). They have the power to give life through encouragement and honesty or to crush and kill through lies and gossip. How can we be assured of producing good words that have a positive outcome? The only way is by diligently guarding our hearts: "Above all else, guard your heart, for everything you do flows from it" (4:23).

Jesus can transform our hearts so that our words can truly be their best—honest, calm, appropriate, and suitable for every situation.

—MARVIN WILLIAMS

Our words have the power to build up or tear down.

²Desire without knowledge is not good —
　　how much more will hasty feet miss the way!

³A person's own folly leads to their ruin,
　　yet their heart rages against the LORD.

⁴Wealth attracts many friends,
　　but even the closest friend of the poor person deserts
　　　them.

⁵A false witness will not go unpunished,
　　and whoever pours out lies will not go free.

⁶Many curry favor with a ruler,
　　and everyone is the friend of one who gives gifts.

⁷The poor are shunned by all their relatives —
　　how much more do their friends avoid them!
Though the poor pursue them with pleading,
　　they are nowhere to be found.^a

⁸The one who gets wisdom loves life;
　　the one who cherishes understanding will soon
　　　prosper.

⁹A false witness will not go unpunished,
　　and whoever pours out lies will perish.

¹⁰It is not fitting for a fool to live in luxury —
　　how much worse for a slave to rule over princes!

¹¹A person's wisdom yields patience;
　　it is to one's glory to overlook an offense.

¹²A king's rage is like the roar of a lion,
　　but his favor is like dew on the grass.

---

^a 7 The meaning of the Hebrew for this sentence is uncertain.

¹³A foolish child is a father's ruin,
  and a quarrelsome wife is like
  the constant dripping of a leaky roof.

¹⁴Houses and wealth are inherited from parents,
  but a prudent wife is from the LORD.

¹⁵Laziness brings on deep sleep,
  and the shiftless go hungry.

¹⁶Whoever keeps commandments keeps their life,
  but whoever shows contempt for their ways will die.

¹⁷Whoever is kind to the poor lends to the LORD,
  and he will reward them for what they have done.

¹⁸Discipline your children, for in that there is hope;
  do not be a willing party to their death.

¹⁹A hot-tempered person must pay the penalty;
  rescue them, and you will have to do it again.

²⁰Listen to advice and accept discipline,
  and at the end you will be counted among the wise.

²¹Many are the plans in a person's heart,
  but it is the LORD's purpose that prevails.

²²What a person desires is unfailing love*ª*;
  better to be poor than a liar.

²³The fear of the LORD leads to life;
  then one rests content, untouched by trouble.

²⁴A sluggard buries his hand in the dish;
  he will not even bring it back to his mouth!

²⁵Flog a mocker, and the simple will learn prudence;
  rebuke the discerning, and they will gain knowledge.

ª 22 Or *Greed is a person's shame*

²⁶Whoever robs their father and drives out their mother
    is a child who brings shame and disgrace.

²⁷Stop listening to instruction, my son,
    and you will stray from the words of knowledge.

²⁸A corrupt witness mocks at justice,
    and the mouth of the wicked gulps down evil.

²⁹Penalties are prepared for mockers,
    and beatings for the backs of fools.

20 Wine is a mocker and beer a brawler;
    whoever is led astray by them is not wise.

²A king's wrath strikes terror like the roar of a lion;
    those who anger him forfeit their lives.

³It is to one's honor to avoid strife,
    but every fool is quick to quarrel.

⁴Sluggards do not plow in season;
    so at harvest time they look but find nothing.

⁵The purposes of a person's heart are deep waters,
    but one who has insight draws them out.

⁶Many claim to have unfailing love,
    but a faithful person who can find?

⁷The righteous lead blameless lives;
    blessed are their children after them.

⁸When a king sits on his throne to judge,
    he winnows out all evil with his eyes.

⁹Who can say, "I have kept my heart pure;
    I am clean and without sin"?

¹⁰Differing weights and differing measures —
the LORD detests them both.

¹¹Even small children are known by their actions,
so is their conduct really pure and upright?

¹²Ears that hear and eyes that see —
the LORD has made them both.

¹³Do not love sleep or you will grow poor;
stay awake and you will have food to spare.

¹⁴"It's no good, it's no good!" says the buyer —
then goes off and boasts about the purchase.

¹⁵Gold there is, and rubies in abundance,
but lips that speak knowledge are a rare jewel.

¹⁶Take the garment of one who puts up security for a
stranger;
hold it in pledge if it is done for an outsider.

¹⁷Food gained by fraud tastes sweet,
but one ends up with a mouth full of gravel.

¹⁸Plans are established by seeking advice;
so if you wage war, obtain guidance.

¹⁹A gossip betrays a confidence;
so avoid anyone who talks too much.

²⁰If someone curses their father or mother,
their lamp will be snuffed out in pitch darkness.

²¹An inheritance claimed too soon
will not be blessed at the end.

²²Do not say, "I'll pay you back for this wrong!"
Wait for the LORD, and he will avenge you.

²³The LORD detests differing weights,
and dishonest scales do not please him.

²⁴A person's steps are directed by the LORD.
How then can anyone understand their own way?

²⁵It is a trap to dedicate something rashly
and only later to consider one's vows.

²⁶A wise king winnows out the wicked;
he drives the threshing wheel over them.

²⁷The human spirit is[a] the lamp of the LORD
that sheds light on one's inmost being.

²⁸Love and faithfulness keep a king safe;
through love his throne is made secure.

²⁹The glory of young men is their strength,
gray hair the splendor of the old.

³⁰Blows and wounds scrub away evil,
and beatings purge the inmost being.

21 In the LORD's hand the king's heart is a stream of water
that he channels toward all who please him.

²A person may think their own ways are right,
but the LORD weighs the heart.

³To do what is right and just
is more acceptable to the LORD than sacrifice.

⁴Haughty eyes and a proud heart —
the unplowed field of the wicked — produce sin.

⁵The plans of the diligent lead to profit
as surely as haste leads to poverty.

---

[a] 27 Or A person's words are

⁶A fortune made by a lying tongue
  is a fleeting vapor and a deadly snare.ᵃ

⁷The violence of the wicked will drag them away,
  for they refuse to do what is right.

⁸The way of the guilty is devious,
  but the conduct of the innocent is upright.

⁹Better to live on a corner of the roof
  than share a house with a quarrelsome wife.

¹⁰The wicked crave evil;
  their neighbors get no mercy from them.

¹¹When a mocker is punished, the simple gain wisdom;
  by paying attention to the wise they get knowledge.

¹²The Righteous Oneᵇ takes note of the house of the wicked
  and brings the wicked to ruin.

¹³Whoever shuts their ears to the cry of the poor
  will also cry out and not be answered.

¹⁴A gift given in secret soothes anger,
  and a bribe concealed in the cloak pacifies great wrath.

¹⁵When justice is done, it brings joy to the righteous
  but terror to evildoers.

¹⁶Whoever strays from the path of prudence
  comes to rest in the company of the dead.

¹⁷Whoever loves pleasure will become poor;
  whoever loves wine and olive oil will never be rich.

¹⁸The wicked become a ransom for the righteous,
  and the unfaithful for the upright.

ᵃ 6 Some Hebrew manuscripts, Septuagint and Vulgate; most Hebrew
manuscripts *vapor for those who seek death*   ᵇ 12 Or *The righteous person*

¹⁹Better to live in a desert
than with a quarrelsome and nagging wife.

²⁰The wise store up choice food and olive oil,
but fools gulp theirs down.

²¹Whoever pursues righteousness and love
finds life, prosperity*a* and honor.

²²One who is wise can go up against the city of the mighty
and pull down the stronghold in which they trust.

²³Those who guard their mouths and their tongues
keep themselves from calamity.

²⁴The proud and arrogant person — "Mocker" is his name —
behaves with insolent fury.

²⁵The craving of a sluggard will be the death of him,
because his hands refuse to work.

²⁶All day long he craves for more,
but the righteous give without sparing.

²⁷The sacrifice of the wicked is detestable —
how much more so when brought with evil intent!

²⁸A false witness will perish,
but a careful listener will testify successfully.

²⁹The wicked put up a bold front,
but the upright give thought to their ways.

³⁰There is no wisdom, no insight, no plan
that can succeed against the LORD.

³¹The horse is made ready for the day of battle,
but victory rests with the LORD.

---

a 21 Or *righteousness*

22 A good name is more desirable than great riches;
to be esteemed is better than silver or gold.

²Rich and poor have this in common:
The Lord is the Maker of them all.

³The prudent see danger and take refuge,
but the simple keep going and pay the penalty.

⁴Humility is the fear of the Lord;
its wages are riches and honor and life.

⁵In the paths of the wicked are snares and pitfalls,
but those who would preserve their life stay far from them.

⁶Start children off on the way they should go,
and even when they are old they will not turn from it.

⁷The rich rule over the poor,
and the borrower is slave to the lender.

⁸Whoever sows injustice reaps calamity,
and the rod they wield in fury will be broken.

⁹The generous will themselves be blessed,
for they share their food with the poor.

¹⁰Drive out the mocker, and out goes strife;
quarrels and insults are ended.

¹¹One who loves a pure heart and who speaks with grace
will have the king for a friend.

¹²The eyes of the Lord keep watch over knowledge,
but he frustrates the words of the unfaithful.

¹³The sluggard says, "There's a lion outside!
I'll be killed in the public square!"

Lessons for Little Ones

Start children off on the way they should go,
and even when they are old they will not turn from it.
PROVERBS 22:6

When my daughter described a problem she was having in the school lunchroom, I immediately wondered how I could fix the issue for her. But then another thought occurred. Maybe God had allowed the problem so she could see Him at work and get to know Him better. Instead of running to the rescue, I decided to pray with her. The trouble cleared up without any help from me!

This situation showed my little one that God cares for her, that He listens when she prays, and that He answers prayers. The Bible says there's something significant about learning these lessons early in life. If we "start children off on the way they should go, . . . when they are old they will not turn from it" (Proverbs 22:6). When we start kids off with an awareness of Jesus and His power, we are giving them a place to return to if they wander and a foundation for spiritual growth throughout their lives.

Consider how you might foster faith in a child. Point out God's design in nature, tell a story about how He has helped you, or invite a little one to thank God with you when things go right. God can work through you to tell of His goodness throughout all generations.

—JENNIFER BENSON SCHULDT

We influence future generations by living for Christ today.

¹⁴The mouth of an adulterous woman is a deep pit;
a man who is under the Lᴏʀᴅ's wrath falls into it.

¹⁵Folly is bound up in the heart of a child,
but the rod of discipline will drive it far away.

¹⁶One who oppresses the poor to increase his wealth
and one who gives gifts to the rich — both come to
poverty.

Thirty Sayings of the Wise

Saying 1

¹⁷Pay attention and turn your ear to the sayings of the wise;
apply your heart to what I teach,

¹⁸for it is pleasing when you keep them in your heart
and have all of them ready on your lips.

¹⁹So that your trust may be in the Lᴏʀᴅ,
I teach you today, even you.

²⁰Have I not written thirty sayings for you,
sayings of counsel and knowledge,

²¹teaching you to be honest and to speak the truth,
so that you bring back truthful reports
to those you serve?

Saying 2

²²Do not exploit the poor because they are poor
and do not crush the needy in court,

²³for the Lᴏʀᴅ will take up their case
and will exact life for life.

Saying 3

²⁴Do not make friends with a hot-tempered person,
do not associate with one easily angered,

[25] or you may learn their ways
  and get yourself ensnared.

Saying 4
[26] Do not be one who shakes hands in pledge
  or puts up security for debts;
[27] if you lack the means to pay,
  your very bed will be snatched from under you.

Saying 5
[28] Do not move an ancient boundary stone
  set up by your ancestors.

Saying 6
[29] Do you see someone skilled in their work?
  They will serve before kings;
  they will not serve before officials of low rank.

Saying 7
23 When you sit to dine with a ruler,
  note well what[a] is before you,
[2] and put a knife to your throat
  if you are given to gluttony.
[3] Do not crave his delicacies,
  for that food is deceptive.

Saying 8
[4] Do not wear yourself out to get rich;
  do not trust your own cleverness.
[5] Cast but a glance at riches, and they are gone,
  for they will surely sprout wings
  and fly off to the sky like an eagle.

[a] 1 Or who

Saying 9

[6]Do not eat the food of a begrudging host,
 do not crave his delicacies;
[7]for he is the kind of person
 who is always thinking about the cost.[a]
"Eat and drink," he says to you,
 but his heart is not with you.
[8]You will vomit up the little you have eaten
 and will have wasted your compliments.

Saying 10

[9]Do not speak to fools,
 for they will scorn your prudent words.

Saying 11

[10]Do not move an ancient boundary stone
 or encroach on the fields of the fatherless,
[11]for their Defender is strong;
 he will take up their case against you.

Saying 12

[12]Apply your heart to instruction
 and your ears to words of knowledge.

Saying 13

[13]Do not withhold discipline from a child;
 if you punish them with the rod, they will not die.
[14]Punish them with the rod
 and save them from death.

---

[a] 7 Or *for as he thinks within himself, / so he is*; or *for as he puts on a feast, / so he is*

Saying 14

[15]My son, if your heart is wise,
then my heart will be glad indeed;
[16]my inmost being will rejoice
when your lips speak what is right.

Saying 15

[17]Do not let your heart envy sinners,
but always be zealous for the fear of the LORD.
[18]There is surely a future hope for you,
and your hope will not be cut off.

Saying 16

[19]Listen, my son, and be wise,
and set your heart on the right path:
[20]Do not join those who drink too much wine
or gorge themselves on meat,
[21]for drunkards and gluttons become poor,
and drowsiness clothes them in rags.

Saying 17

[22]Listen to your father, who gave you life,
and do not despise your mother when she is old.
[23]Buy the truth and do not sell it —
wisdom, instruction and insight as well.
[24]The father of a righteous child has great joy;
a man who fathers a wise son rejoices in him.
[25]May your father and mother rejoice;
may she who gave you birth be joyful!

Saying 18

[26]My son, give me your heart
and let your eyes delight in my ways,

[27] for an adulterous woman is a deep pit,
   and a wayward wife is a narrow well.
[28] Like a bandit she lies in wait
   and multiplies the unfaithful among men.

Saying 19
[29] Who has woe? Who has sorrow?
   Who has strife? Who has complaints?
   Who has needless bruises? Who has bloodshot eyes?
[30] Those who linger over wine,
   who go to sample bowls of mixed wine.
[31] Do not gaze at wine when it is red,
   when it sparkles in the cup,
   when it goes down smoothly!
[32] In the end it bites like a snake
   and poisons like a viper.
[33] Your eyes will see strange sights,
   and your mind will imagine confusing things.
[34] You will be like one sleeping on the high seas,
   lying on top of the rigging.
[35] "They hit me," you will say, "but I'm not hurt!
   They beat me, but I don't feel it!
   When will I wake up
   so I can find another drink?"

Saying 20
24 Do not envy the wicked,
   do not desire their company;
[2] for their hearts plot violence,
   and their lips talk about making trouble.

Saying 21
³By wisdom a house is built,
  and through understanding it is established;
⁴through knowledge its rooms are filled
  with rare and beautiful treasures.

Saying 22
⁵The wise prevail through great power,
  and those who have knowledge muster their strength.
⁶Surely you need guidance to wage war,
  and victory is won through many advisers.

Saying 23
⁷Wisdom is too high for fools;
  in the assembly at the gate they must not open their
    mouths.

Saying 24
⁸Whoever plots evil
  will be known as a schemer.
⁹The schemes of folly are sin,
  and people detest a mocker.

Saying 25
¹⁰If you falter in a time of trouble,
  how small is your strength!
¹¹Rescue those being led away to death;
  hold back those staggering toward slaughter.
¹²If you say, "But we knew nothing about this,"
  does not he who weighs the heart perceive it?
  Does not he who guards your life know it?

>   Will he not repay everyone according to what they
>   have done?

Saying 26
[13] Eat honey, my son, for it is good;
>   honey from the comb is sweet to your taste.
[14] Know also that wisdom is like honey for you:
>   If you find it, there is a future hope for you,
>   and your hope will not be cut off.

Saying 27
[15] Do not lurk like a thief near the house of the righteous,
>   do not plunder their dwelling place;
[16] for though the righteous fall seven times, they rise again,
>   but the wicked stumble when calamity strikes.

Saying 28
[17] Do not gloat when your enemy falls;
>   when they stumble, do not let your heart rejoice,
[18] or the LORD will see and disapprove
>   and turn his wrath away from them.

Saying 29
[19] Do not fret because of evildoers
>   or be envious of the wicked,
[20] for the evildoer has no future hope,
>   and the lamp of the wicked will be snuffed out.

Saying 30
[21] Fear the LORD and the king, my son,
>   and do not join with rebellious officials,

²²for those two will send sudden destruction on them,
and who knows what calamities they can bring?

Further Sayings of the Wise

²³These also are sayings of the wise:

To show partiality in judging is not good:
²⁴Whoever says to the guilty, "You are innocent,"
will be cursed by peoples and denounced
by nations.
²⁵But it will go well with those who convict the guilty,
and rich blessing will come on them.

²⁶An honest answer
is like a kiss on the lips.

²⁷Put your outdoor work in order
and get your fields ready;
after that, build your house.

²⁸Do not testify against your neighbor without cause —
would you use your lips to mislead?
²⁹Do not say, "I'll do to them as they have done to me;
I'll pay them back for what they did."

³⁰I went past the field of a sluggard,
past the vineyard of someone who has no sense;
³¹thorns had come up everywhere,
the ground was covered with weeds,
and the stone wall was in ruins.
³²I applied my heart to what I observed
and learned a lesson from what I saw:
³³A little sleep, a little slumber,
a little folding of the hands to rest —

³⁴and poverty will come on you like a thief
   and scarcity like an armed man.

More Proverbs of Solomon

25 These are more proverbs of Solomon, compiled by the men of Hezekiah king of Judah:

²It is the glory of God to conceal a matter;
   to search out a matter is the glory of kings.
³As the heavens are high and the earth is deep,
   so the hearts of kings are unsearchable.

⁴Remove the dross from the silver,
   and a silversmith can produce a vessel;
⁵remove wicked officials from the king's presence,
   and his throne will be established through
      righteousness.

⁶Do not exalt yourself in the king's presence,
   and do not claim a place among his great men;
⁷it is better for him to say to you, "Come up here,"
   than for him to humiliate you before his nobles.

What you have seen with your eyes
⁸   do not bring*ᵃ* hastily to court,
for what will you do in the end
   if your neighbor puts you to shame?

⁹If you take your neighbor to court,
   do not betray another's confidence,
¹⁰or the one who hears it may shame you
   and the charge against you will stand.

ᵃ 7,8 Or nobles / on whom you had set your eyes. / ⁸Do not go

¹¹Like apples^{*a*} of gold in settings of silver
    is a ruling rightly given.
¹²Like an earring of gold or an ornament of fine gold
    is the rebuke of a wise judge to a listening ear.

¹³Like a snow-cooled drink at harvest time
    is a trustworthy messenger to the one who sends him;
    he refreshes the spirit of his master.
¹⁴Like clouds and wind without rain
    is one who boasts of gifts never given.

¹⁵Through patience a ruler can be persuaded,
    and a gentle tongue can break a bone.

¹⁶If you find honey, eat just enough —
    too much of it, and you will vomit.
¹⁷Seldom set foot in your neighbor's house —
    too much of you, and they will hate you.

¹⁸Like a club or a sword or a sharp arrow
    is one who gives false testimony against a neighbor.
¹⁹Like a broken tooth or a lame foot
    is reliance on the unfaithful in a time of trouble.
²⁰Like one who takes away a garment on a cold day,
    or like vinegar poured on a wound,
    is one who sings songs to a heavy heart.

²¹If your enemy is hungry, give him food to eat;
    if he is thirsty, give him water to drink.
²²In doing this, you will heap burning coals on his head,
    and the LORD will reward you.

²³Like a north wind that brings unexpected rain
    is a sly tongue — which provokes a horrified look.

---

^{*a*} *11* Or possibly *apricots*

²⁴Better to live on a corner of the roof
 than share a house with a quarrelsome wife.

²⁵Like cold water to a weary soul
 is good news from a distant land.
²⁶Like a muddied spring or a polluted well
 are the righteous who give way to the wicked.

²⁷It is not good to eat too much honey,
 nor is it honorable to search out matters that are too
  deep.

²⁸Like a city whose walls are broken through
 is a person who lacks self-control.

26 Like snow in summer or rain in harvest,
 honor is not fitting for a fool.
²Like a fluttering sparrow or a darting swallow,
 an undeserved curse does not come to rest.
³A whip for the horse, a bridle for the donkey,
 and a rod for the backs of fools!
⁴Do not answer a fool according to his folly,
 or you yourself will be just like him.
⁵Answer a fool according to his folly,
 or he will be wise in his own eyes.
⁶Sending a message by the hands of a fool
 is like cutting off one's feet or drinking poison.
⁷Like the useless legs of one who is lame
 is a proverb in the mouth of a fool.
⁸Like tying a stone in a sling
 is the giving of honor to a fool.
⁹Like a thornbush in a drunkard's hand
 is a proverb in the mouth of a fool.

¹⁰Like an archer who wounds at random
  is one who hires a fool or any passer-by.
¹¹As a dog returns to its vomit,
  so fools repeat their folly.
¹²Do you see a person wise in their own eyes?
  There is more hope for a fool than for them.

¹³A sluggard says, "There's a lion in the road,
  a fierce lion roaming the streets!"
¹⁴As a door turns on its hinges,
  so a sluggard turns on his bed.
¹⁵A sluggard buries his hand in the dish;
  he is too lazy to bring it back to his mouth.
¹⁶A sluggard is wiser in his own eyes
  than seven people who answer discreetly.

¹⁷Like one who grabs a stray dog by the ears
  is someone who rushes into a quarrel not their own.

¹⁸Like a maniac shooting
  flaming arrows of death
¹⁹is one who deceives their neighbor
  and says, "I was only joking!"

²⁰Without wood a fire goes out;
  without a gossip a quarrel dies down.
²¹As charcoal to embers and as wood to fire,
  so is a quarrelsome person for kindling strife.
²²The words of a gossip are like choice morsels;
  they go down to the inmost parts.

²³Like a coating of silver dross on earthenware
  are fervent*ᵃ* lips with an evil heart.

ᵃ 23 Hebrew; Septuagint *smooth*

²⁴Enemies disguise themselves with their lips,
  but in their hearts they harbor deceit.
²⁵Though their speech is charming, do not believe them,
  for seven abominations fill their hearts.
²⁶Their malice may be concealed by deception,
  but their wickedness will be exposed in the assembly.
²⁷Whoever digs a pit will fall into it;
  if someone rolls a stone, it will roll back on them.
²⁸A lying tongue hates those it hurts,
  and a flattering mouth works ruin.

27 Do not boast about tomorrow,
  for you do not know what a day may bring.

²Let someone else praise you, and not your own mouth;
  an outsider, and not your own lips.

³Stone is heavy and sand a burden,
  but a fool's provocation is heavier than both.

⁴Anger is cruel and fury overwhelming,
  but who can stand before jealousy?

⁵Better is open rebuke
  than hidden love.

⁶Wounds from a friend can be trusted,
  but an enemy multiplies kisses.

⁷One who is full loathes honey from the comb,
  but to the hungry even what is bitter tastes sweet.

⁸Like a bird that flees its nest
  is anyone who flees from home.

Wounds from a Friend

Wounds from a friend can be trusted.
PROVERBS 27:6

Charles Lowery complained to his friend about lower back pain. He was seeking a sympathetic ear, but what he got was an honest assessment. His friend told him, "I don't think your back pain is your problem; it's your stomach. Your stomach is so big it's pulling on your back."

In his column for national magazine, Lowerey shared that he resisted the temptation to be offended. He lost the weight and his back problem went away. Lowery recognized that "Better is open rebuke than hidden love. Wounds from a friend can be trusted" (Proverbs 27:5–6).

The trouble is that so often we would rather be ruined by praise than saved by criticism, for truth hurts. It bruises our ego, makes us uncomfortable, and calls for change.

True friends don't find pleasure in hurting us. Rather, they love us too much to deceive us. They are people who, with loving courage, point out what we may already know but find hard to truly accept and live by. They tell us not only what we like to hear but also what we need to hear.

Solomon honored such friendship in his proverbs. Jesus went further—He endured the wounds of our rejection not only to tell us the truth about ourselves but also to show us how much we are loved.

—POH FANG CHIA

A friend is one who can tell you the truth in love.

⁹Perfume and incense bring joy to the heart,
    and the pleasantness of a friend
    springs from their heartfelt advice.

¹⁰Do not forsake your friend or a friend of your family,
    and do not go to your relative's house when disaster
        strikes you —
    better a neighbor nearby than a relative far away.

¹¹Be wise, my son, and bring joy to my heart;
    then I can answer anyone who treats me with
        contempt.

¹²The prudent see danger and take refuge,
    but the simple keep going and pay the penalty.

¹³Take the garment of one who puts up security for a
        stranger;
    hold it in pledge if it is done for an outsider.

¹⁴If anyone loudly blesses their neighbor early in the
        morning,
    it will be taken as a curse.

¹⁵A quarrelsome wife is like the dripping
    of a leaky roof in a rainstorm;
¹⁶restraining her is like restraining the wind
    or grasping oil with the hand.

¹⁷As iron sharpens iron,
    so one person sharpens another.

¹⁸The one who guards a fig tree will eat its fruit,
    and whoever protects their master will be honored.

¹⁹As water reflects the face,
    so one's life reflects the heart. [a]

---

[a] 19 Or *so others reflect your heart back to you*

²⁰Death and Destruction*a* are never satisfied,
and neither are human eyes.

²¹The crucible for silver and the furnace for gold,
but people are tested by their praise.

²²Though you grind a fool in a mortar,
grinding them like grain with a pestle,
you will not remove their folly from them.

²³Be sure you know the condition of your flocks,
give careful attention to your herds;
²⁴for riches do not endure forever,
and a crown is not secure for all generations.
²⁵When the hay is removed and new growth appears
and the grass from the hills is gathered in,
²⁶the lambs will provide you with clothing,
and the goats with the price of a field.
²⁷You will have plenty of goats' milk to feed your family
and to nourish your female servants.

28 The wicked flee though no one pursues,
but the righteous are as bold as a lion.

²When a country is rebellious, it has many rulers,
but a ruler with discernment and knowledge
maintains order.

³A ruler*b* who oppresses the poor
is like a driving rain that leaves no crops.

⁴Those who forsake instruction praise the wicked,
but those who heed it resist them.

⁵Evildoers do not understand what is right,
but those who seek the LORD understand it fully.

---

a 20 Hebrew *Abaddon*   *b* 3 Or *A poor person*

⁶Better the poor whose walk is blameless
    than the rich whose ways are perverse.

⁷A discerning son heeds instruction,
    but a companion of gluttons disgraces his father.

⁸Whoever increases wealth by taking interest or profit
      from the poor
    amasses it for another, who will be kind to the poor.

⁹If anyone turns a deaf ear to my instruction,
    even their prayers are detestable.

¹⁰Whoever leads the upright along an evil path
    will fall into their own trap,
    but the blameless will receive a good inheritance.

¹¹The rich are wise in their own eyes;
    one who is poor and discerning sees how deluded
      they are.

¹²When the righteous triumph, there is great elation;
    but when the wicked rise to power, people go into
      hiding.

¹³Whoever conceals their sins does not prosper,
    but the one who confesses and renounces them finds
      mercy.

¹⁴Blessed is the one who always trembles before God,
    but whoever hardens their heart falls into trouble.

¹⁵Like a roaring lion or a charging bear
    is a wicked ruler over a helpless people.

¹⁶A tyrannical ruler practices extortion,
    but one who hates ill-gotten gain will enjoy a long reign.

¹⁷Anyone tormented by the guilt of murder
  will seek refuge in the grave;
  let no one hold them back.

¹⁸The one whose walk is blameless is kept safe,
  but the one whose ways are perverse will fall into
    the pit.ᵃ

¹⁹Those who work their land will have abundant food,
  but those who chase fantasies will have their fill of
    poverty.

²⁰A faithful person will be richly blessed,
  but one eager to get rich will not go unpunished.

²¹To show partiality is not good —
  yet a person will do wrong for a piece of bread.

²²The stingy are eager to get rich
  and are unaware that poverty awaits them.

²³Whoever rebukes a person will in the end gain favor
  rather than one who has a flattering tongue.

²⁴Whoever robs their father or mother
  and says, "It's not wrong,"
  is partner to one who destroys.

²⁵The greedy stir up conflict,
  but those who trust in the LORD will prosper.

²⁶Those who trust in themselves are fools,
  but those who walk in wisdom are kept safe.

²⁷Those who give to the poor will lack nothing,
  but those who close their eyes to them receive many
    curses.

ᵃ 18 Syriac (see Septuagint); Hebrew *into one*

²⁸When the wicked rise to power, people go into hiding;
  but when the wicked perish, the righteous thrive.

29 Whoever remains stiff-necked after many rebukes
    will suddenly be destroyed — without remedy.

²When the righteous thrive, the people rejoice;
  when the wicked rule, the people groan.

³A man who loves wisdom brings joy to his father,
  but a companion of prostitutes squanders his wealth.

⁴By justice a king gives a country stability,
  but those who are greedy for*ᵃ* bribes tear it down.

⁵Those who flatter their neighbors
  are spreading nets for their feet.

⁶Evildoers are snared by their own sin,
  but the righteous shout for joy and are glad.

⁷The righteous care about justice for the poor,
  but the wicked have no such concern.

⁸Mockers stir up a city,
  but the wise turn away anger.

⁹If a wise person goes to court with a fool,
  the fool rages and scoffs, and there is no peace.

¹⁰The bloodthirsty hate a person of integrity
  and seek to kill the upright.

¹¹Fools give full vent to their rage,
  but the wise bring calm in the end.

¹²If a ruler listens to lies,
  all his officials become wicked.

———————

ᵃ 4 Or *who give*

¹³The poor and the oppressor have this in common:
  The LORD gives sight to the eyes of both.

¹⁴If a king judges the poor with fairness,
  his throne will be established forever.

¹⁵A rod and a reprimand impart wisdom,
  but a child left undisciplined disgraces its mother.

¹⁶When the wicked thrive, so does sin,
  but the righteous will see their downfall.

¹⁷Discipline your children, and they will give you peace;
  they will bring you the delights you desire.

¹⁸Where there is no revelation, people cast off restraint;
  but blessed is the one who heeds wisdom's instruction.

¹⁹Servants cannot be corrected by mere words;
  though they understand, they will not respond.

²⁰Do you see someone who speaks in haste?
  There is more hope for a fool than for them.

²¹A servant pampered from youth
  will turn out to be insolent.

²²An angry person stirs up conflict,
  and a hot-tempered person commits many sins.

²³Pride brings a person low,
  but the lowly in spirit gain honor.

²⁴The accomplices of thieves are their own enemies;
  they are put under oath and dare not testify.

²⁵Fear of man will prove to be a snare,
  but whoever trusts in the LORD is kept safe.

²⁶Many seek an audience with a ruler,
  but it is from the LORD that one gets justice.

²⁷The righteous detest the dishonest;
the wicked detest the upright.

Sayings of Agur

30 The sayings of Agur son of Jakeh — an inspired
utterance.

This man's utterance to Ithiel:

"I am weary, God,
but I can prevail.ᵃ
²Surely I am only a brute, not a man;
I do not have human understanding.
³I have not learned wisdom,
nor have I attained to the knowledge of the Holy One.
⁴Who has gone up to heaven and come down?
Whose hands have gathered up the wind?
Who has wrapped up the waters in a cloak?
Who has established all the ends of the earth?
What is his name, and what is the name of his son?
Surely you know!

⁵"Every word of God is flawless;
he is a shield to those who take refuge in him.
⁶Do not add to his words,
or he will rebuke you and prove you a liar.

⁷"Two things I ask of you, LORD;
do not refuse me before I die:
⁸Keep falsehood and lies far from me;
give me neither poverty nor riches,
but give me only my daily bread.

ᵃ *1* With a different word division of the Hebrew; Masoretic Text *utterance to
Ithiel, / to Ithiel and Ukal:*

⁹Otherwise, I may have too much and disown you
    and say, 'Who is the LORD?'
Or I may become poor and steal,
    and so dishonor the name of my God.

¹⁰"Do not slander a servant to their master,
    or they will curse you, and you will pay for it.

¹¹"There are those who curse their fathers
    and do not bless their mothers;
¹²those who are pure in their own eyes
    and yet are not cleansed of their filth;
¹³those whose eyes are ever so haughty,
    whose glances are so disdainful;
¹⁴those whose teeth are swords
    and whose jaws are set with knives
to devour the poor from the earth
    and the needy from among mankind.

¹⁵"The leech has two daughters.
    'Give! Give!' they cry.

"There are three things that are never satisfied,
    four that never say, 'Enough!':
¹⁶the grave, the barren womb,
    land, which is never satisfied with water,
    and fire, which never says, 'Enough!'

¹⁷"The eye that mocks a father,
    that scorns an aged mother,
will be pecked out by the ravens of the valley,
    will be eaten by the vultures.

¹⁸"There are three things that are too amazing for me,
    four that I do not understand:

¹⁹ the way of an eagle in the sky,
    the way of a snake on a rock,
  the way of a ship on the high seas,
    and the way of a man with a young woman.

²⁰ "This is the way of an adulterous woman:
    She eats and wipes her mouth
    and says, 'I've done nothing wrong.'

²¹ "Under three things the earth trembles,
    under four it cannot bear up:
²² a servant who becomes king,
    a godless fool who gets plenty to eat,
²³ a contemptible woman who gets married,
    and a servant who displaces her mistress.

²⁴ "Four things on earth are small,
    yet they are extremely wise:
²⁵ Ants are creatures of little strength,
    yet they store up their food in the summer;
²⁶ hyraxes are creatures of little power,
    yet they make their home in the crags;
²⁷ locusts have no king,
    yet they advance together in ranks;
²⁸ a lizard can be caught with the hand,
    yet it is found in kings' palaces.

²⁹ "There are three things that are stately in their stride,
    four that move with stately bearing:
³⁰ a lion, mighty among beasts,
    who retreats before nothing;
³¹ a strutting rooster, a he-goat,
    and a king secure against revolt.^a

---

^a *31* The meaning of the Hebrew for this phrase is uncertain.

The Bug Zoo

Ants are creatures of little strength,
yet they store up their food in the summer.
PROVERBS 30:25

A bug zoo in Philadelphia with more than 100,000 live insects entertains 75,000 visitors a year. The Insectarium's founder and proprietor says, "I've got a million more bugs still in storage." He points to boxes, cookie tins, and other containers piled floor-to-ceiling, filled with dead bugs from around the globe. Movies, holograms, microscopes, and games keep people of all ages occupied. There's even a scale to weigh yourself in ladybugs, fireflies, and other creatures.

In Proverbs 30, a wise man named Agur also showcases insects and other small creatures. He calls them small but very wise.

Look at the ant. He's weak, but his Creator has taught him to use whatever strength he has to prepare for the future. Consider the locust. He has no king, but when his numbers multiply, God has taught him how to line up and move as one. Look at the lizard. He too is a lowly creature, but by using the ability God gives him, he rises to high places.

Do you sometimes feel small and insignificant like an insect? When you do, remember that God showcases His wisdom and greatness through even the smallest things. That's because His "power is made perfect in weakness" (2 Corinthians 12:9).

—MART DEHAAN

God's wisdom is given to those who humbly ask Him for it.

[32] "If you play the fool and exalt yourself,
    or if you plan evil,
    clap your hand over your mouth!
[33] For as churning cream produces butter,
    and as twisting the nose produces blood,
    so stirring up anger produces strife."

Sayings of King Lemuel

31 The sayings of King Lemuel — an inspired utterance
    his mother taught him.

[2] Listen, my son! Listen, son of my womb!
    Listen, my son, the answer to my prayers!
[3] Do not spend your strength[a] on women,
    your vigor on those who ruin kings.

[4] It is not for kings, Lemuel —
    it is not for kings to drink wine,
    not for rulers to crave beer,
[5] lest they drink and forget what has been decreed,
    and deprive all the oppressed of their rights.
[6] Let beer be for those who are perishing,
    wine for those who are in anguish!
[7] Let them drink and forget their poverty
    and remember their misery no more.

[8] Speak up for those who cannot speak for themselves,
    for the rights of all who are destitute.
[9] Speak up and judge fairly;
    defend the rights of the poor and needy.

---

[a] 3 Or *wealth*

Epilogue: The Wife of Noble Character

[10a]A wife of noble character who can find?
 She is worth far more than rubies.
[11]Her husband has full confidence in her
 and lacks nothing of value.
[12]She brings him good, not harm,
 all the days of her life.
[13]She selects wool and flax
 and works with eager hands.
[14]She is like the merchant ships,
 bringing her food from afar.
[15]She gets up while it is still night;
 she provides food for her family
 and portions for her female servants.
[16]She considers a field and buys it;
 out of her earnings she plants a vineyard.
[17]She sets about her work vigorously;
 her arms are strong for her tasks.
[18]She sees that her trading is profitable,
 and her lamp does not go out at night.
[19]In her hand she holds the distaff
 and grasps the spindle with her fingers.
[20]She opens her arms to the poor
 and extends her hands to the needy.
[21]When it snows, she has no fear for her household;
 for all of them are clothed in scarlet.
[22]She makes coverings for her bed;
 she is clothed in fine linen and purple.

---

[a] 10 Verses 10-31 are an acrostic poem, the verses of which begin with the successive letters of the Hebrew alphabet.

²³Her husband is respected at the city gate,
   where he takes his seat among the elders of the land.
²⁴She makes linen garments and sells them,
   and supplies the merchants with sashes.
²⁵She is clothed with strength and dignity;
   she can laugh at the days to come.
²⁶She speaks with wisdom,
   and faithful instruction is on her tongue.
²⁷She watches over the affairs of her household
   and does not eat the bread of idleness.
²⁸Her children arise and call her blessed;
   her husband also, and he praises her:
²⁹"Many women do noble things,
   but you surpass them all."
³⁰Charm is deceptive, and beauty is fleeting;
   but a woman who fears the LORD is to be praised.
³¹Honor her for all that her hands have done,
   and let her works bring her praise at the city gate.

About the NIV

The goal of the New International Version (NIV) is to enable English-speaking people from around the world to read and hear God's eternal Word in their own language. Our work as translators is motivated by our conviction that the Bible is God's Word in written form. We believe that the Bible contains the divine answer to the deepest needs of humanity, sheds unique light on our path in a dark world and sets forth the way to our eternal well-being. Out of these deep convictions, we have sought to recreate as far as possible the experience of the original audience—blending transparency to the original text with accessibility for the millions of English speakers around the world. We have prioritized accuracy, clarity and literary quality with the goal of creating a translation suitable for public and private reading, evangelism, teaching, preaching, memorizing and liturgical use. We have also sought to preserve a measure of continuity with the long tradition of translating the Scriptures into English.

The complete NIV Bible was first published in 1978. It was a completely new translation made by over a hundred scholars working directly from the best available Hebrew, Aramaic and Greek texts. The translators came from the United States, Great Britain, Canada, Australia and New Zealand, giving the translation an international scope. They were from many denominations and churches — including Anglican, Assemblies of God, Baptist, Brethren, Christian Reformed, Church of Christ, Evangelical Covenant, Evangelical Free, Lutheran, Mennonite, Methodist, Nazarene, Presbyterian, Wesleyan and others. This breadth of denominational and theological perspective helped to safeguard the translation from sectarian bias. For these reasons, and by the grace of God, the NIV has gained a wide readership in all parts of the English-speaking world.

The work of translating the Bible is never finished. As good as they are, English translations must be regularly updated so that they will continue to communicate accurately the meaning of God's Word.

Updates are needed in order to reflect the latest developments in our understanding of the biblical world and its languages and to keep pace with changes in English usage. Recognizing, then, that the NIV would retain its ability to communicate God's Word accurately only if it were regularly updated, the original translators established the Committee on Bible Translation (CBT). The Committee is a self-perpetuating group of biblical scholars charged with keeping abreast of advances in biblical scholarship and changes in English and issuing periodic updates to the NIV. The CBT is an independent, self-governing body and has sole responsibility for the NIV text. The Committee mirrors the original group of translators in its diverse international and denominational makeup and in its unifying commitment to the Bible as God's inspired Word.

In obedience to its mandate, the Committee has issued periodic updates to the NIV. An initial revision was released in 1984. A more thorough revision process was completed in 2005, resulting in the separately published TNIV. The updated NIV you now have in your hands builds on both the original NIV and the TNIV and represents the latest effort of the Committee to articulate God's unchanging Word in the way the original authors might have said it had they been speaking in English to the global English-speaking audience today.

Translation Philosophy

The Committee's translating work has been governed by three widely accepted principles about the way people use words and about the way we understand them.

First, the meaning of words is determined by the way that users of the language actually use them at any given time. For the biblical languages, therefore, the Committee utilizes the best and most recent scholarship on the way Hebrew, Aramaic and Greek words were being used in biblical times. At the same time, the Committee carefully studies the state of modern English. Good translation is like good communication: one must know the target audience so that the appropriate choices can be made about which English words to use to represent the original words of Scripture. From its inception, the NIV has had as its target the general English-speaking population all over the world, the "International" in its title reflecting this concern. The aim of the Committee is to put the Scriptures into natural English that will communicate effectively with the broadest possible audience of English speakers.

Modern technology has enhanced the Committee's ability to choose the right English words to convey the meaning of the original text. The field of computational linguistics harnesses the power of computers to provide broadly applicable and current data about the state of the language. Translators can now access huge databases of modern English to better understand the current meaning and usage of key words. The Committee utilized this resource in preparing the 2011 edition of the NIV. An area of especially rapid and significant change in English is the way certain nouns and pronouns are used to refer to human beings. The Committee therefore requested experts in computational linguistics at Collins Dictionaries to pose some key questions about this usage to its database of English—the largest in the world, with over 4.4 billion words, gathered from several English-speaking countries and including both spoken and written English. (The Collins Study, called "The Development and Use of Gender Language in Contemporary English," can be accessed at http://www.thenivbible.com/about-the-niv/about-the-2011-edition.) The study revealed that the most popular words to describe the human race in modern U.S. English were "humanity," "man" and "mankind." The Committee then used this data in the updated NIV, choosing from among these three words (and occasionally others also) depending on the context.

A related issue creates a larger problem for modern translations: the move away from using the third-person masculine singular pronouns—"he/him/his"—to refer to men and women equally. This usage does persist in some forms of English, and this revision therefore occasionally uses these pronouns in a generic sense. But the tendency, recognized in day-to-day usage and confirmed by the Collins study, is away from the generic use of "he," "him" and "his." In recognition of this shift in language and in an effort to translate into the natural English that people are actually using, this revision of the NIV generally uses other constructions when the biblical text is plainly addressed to men and women equally. The reader will encounter especially frequently a "they," "their" or "them" to express a generic singular idea. Thus, for instance, Mark 8:36 reads: "What good is it for someone to gain the whole world, yet forfeit their soul?" This generic use of the "distributive" or "singular" "they/them/their" has been used for many centuries by respected writers of English and has now become established as standard English, spoken and written, all over the world.

A second linguistic principle that feeds into the Committee's translation work is that meaning is found not in individual words, as vital as they are, but in larger clusters: phrases, clauses, sentences, discourses. Translation is not, as many people think, a matter of word substitution: English word *x* in place of Hebrew word *y*. Translators must first determine the meaning of the words of the biblical languages in the context of the passage and then select English words that accurately communicate that meaning to modern listeners and readers. This means that accurate translation will not always reflect the exact structure of the original language. To be sure, there is debate over the degree to which translators should try to preserve the "form" of the original text in English. From the beginning, the NIV has taken a mediating position on this issue. The manual produced when the translation that became the NIV was first being planned states: "If the Greek or Hebrew syntax has a good parallel in modern English, it should be used. But if there is no good parallel, the English syntax appropriate to the meaning of the original is to be chosen." It is fine, in other words, to carry over the form of the biblical languages into English—but not at the expense of natural expression. The principle that meaning resides in larger clusters of words means that the Committee has not insisted on a "word-forword" approach to translation. We certainly believe that every word of Scripture is inspired by God and therefore to be carefully studied to determine what God is saying to us. It is for this reason that the Committee labors over every single word of the original texts, working hard to determine how each of those words contributes to what the text is saying. Ultimately, however, it is how these individual words function in combination with other words that determines meaning.

A third linguistic principle guiding the Committee in its translation work is the recognition that words have a spectrum of meaning. It is popular to define a word by using another word, or "gloss," to substitute for it. This substitute word is then sometimes called the "literal" meaning of a word. In fact, however, words have a range of possible meanings. Those meanings will vary depending on the context, and words in one language will usually not occupy the same semantic range as words in another language. The Committee therefore studies each original word of Scripture in its context to identify its meaning in a particular verse and then chooses an appropriate English word (or phrase) to represent it. It is impossible, then, to translate any given Hebrew, Aramaic or Greek word with the same English word all the time. The Committee does try to translate related occurrences of a word in the original languages with the same English word in order to preserve the connection for the English reader. But the Committee generally privileges clear natural meaning over a concern with consistency in rendering particular words.

Textual Basis

For the Old Testament the standard Hebrew text, the Masoretic Text as published in the latest edition of *Biblia Hebraica*, has been used throughout. The Masoretic Text tradition contains marginal notations that offer variant readings. These have sometimes been followed instead of the text itself. Because such instances involve variants within the Masoretic tradition, they have not been indicated in the textual notes. In a few cases, words in the basic consonantal text have been divided differently than in the Masoretic Text. Such cases are usually indicated in the textual footnotes. The Dead Sea Scrolls contain biblical texts that represent an earlier stage of the transmission of the Hebrew text. They have been consulted, as have been the Samaritan Pentateuch and the ancient scribal traditions concerning deliberate textual changes. The translators also consulted the more important early versions. Readings from these versions, the Dead Sea Scrolls and the scribal traditions were occasionally followed where the Masoretic Text seemed doubtful and where accepted principles of textual criticism showed that one or more of these textual witnesses appeared to provide the correct reading. In rare cases, the translators have emended the Hebrew text where it appears to have become corrupted at an even earlier stage of its transmission. These departures from the Masoretic Text are also indicated in the textual footnotes. Sometimes the vowel indicators (which are later additions to the basic consonantal text) found in the Masoretic Text did not, in the judgment of the translators, represent the correct vowels for the original text. Accordingly, some words have been read with a different set of vowels. These instances are usually not indicated in the footnotes.

The Greek text used in translating the New Testament has been an eclectic one, based on the latest editions of the Nestle-Aland/United Bible Societies' Greek New Testament. The translators have made their choices among the variant readings in accordance with widely accepted principles of New Testament textual criticism. Footnotes call attention to places where uncertainty remains.

The New Testament authors, writing in Greek, often quote the Old Testament from its ancient Greek version, the Septuagint. This is one reason why some of the Old Testament quotations in the NIV New Testament are not identical to the corresponding passages in the NIV Old Testament. Such quotations in the New Testament are indicated with the footnote "(see Septuagint)."

Footnotes and Formatting

Footnotes in this version are of several kinds, most of which need no explanation. Those giving alternative translations begin with "Or" and generally introduce the alternative with the last word preceding it in the text, except when it is a single-word alternative. When poetry is quoted in a footnote a slash mark indicates a line division.

It should be noted that references to diseases, minerals, flora and fauna, architectural details, clothing, jewelry, musical instruments and other articles cannot always be identified with precision. Also, linear measurements and measures of capacity can only be approximated (see the Table of Weights and Measures). Although *Selah*, used mainly in the Psalms, is probably a musical term, its meaning is uncertain. Since it may interrupt reading and distract the reader, this word has not been kept in the English text, but every occurrence has been signaled by a footnote.

As an aid to the reader, sectional headings have been inserted. They are not to be regarded as part of the biblical text and are not intended for oral reading. It is the Committee's hope that these headings may prove more helpful to the reader than the traditional chapter divisions, which were introduced long after the Bible was written.

Sometimes the chapter and/or verse numbering in English translations of the Old Testament differs from that found in published Hebrew texts. This is particularly the case in the Psalms, where the traditional titles are included in the Hebrew verse numbering. Such differences are indicated in the footnotes at the bottom of the page. In the New Testament, verse numbers that marked off portions of the traditional English text not supported by the best Greek manuscripts now appear in brackets, with a footnote indicating the text that has been omitted (see, for example, Matthew 17:[21]).

Mark 16:9-20 and John 7:53–8:11, although long accorded virtually equal status with the rest of the Gospels in which they stand, have a questionable standing in the textual history of the New Testament, as noted in the bracketed annotations with which they are set off. A different typeface has been chosen for these passages to indicate their uncertain status.

Basic formatting of the text, such as lining the poetry, paragraphing (both prose and poetry), setting up of (administrative-like) lists, indenting letters and lengthy prayers within narratives and the insertion of sectional headings, has been the work of the Committee. However, the choice between single-column and double-column formats has been left to the publishers. Also the issuing of "red-letter" editions is a publisher's choice—one that the Committee does not endorse.

The Committee has again been reminded that every human effort is flawed—including this revision of the NIV. We trust, however, that many will find in it an improved representation of the Word of God, through which they hear his call to faith in our Lord Jesus Christ and to service in his kingdom. We offer this version of the Bible to him in whose name and for whose glory it has been made.

The Committee on Bible Translation